6 DOCTORS' VISITS

by Tara Lynn Fulton

Jack and four other people were all at the medical center last week for doctor visits. Each person saw a different physician (one saw Dr. Sands), each of whom has a different specialty (one is an ophthalmologist). From the clues below, can you determine the full name of each patient, and the name and specialty of his or her doctor?

1. Jim Fisk did not go to Dr. Pershy.

2. The three women are the one who visited Dr. Noble, Ms. Falmer, and the one who saw the dermatologist.

3. Ms. Foster visited the surgeon.

4. The orthopedist, who is not French's doctor, is not Dr. Carter.

5. A woman went to Dr. Aronson, but she was not Jean.

6. Janet is not the woman who saw the obstetrician, who is not Dr. Carter.

7. Jill's last name is Furness.

The solution is on page 140.

	Falmer	Fisk	Foster	French	Furness	A.	C.	N.	P.	S.	derm.	obs.	oph.	orth.	sur.
						saw Doctor									
Jack															
Janet															
Jean															
Jill															
Jim															
derm.															
obs.															
oph.															
orth.															
sur.															
Doctor A.															
Doctor C.															
Doctor N.															
Doctor P.															
Doctor S.															

5 THE CRAFT FAIR

by Virginia C. McCarthy

At the annual craft fair six exhibitors, five women and one man, including a glassblower, displayed their works in booths. When the fair ended, they tried to work out agreeable trades with one another. From the following clues, can you determine who is engaged in each craft and who exchanged with whom?

1. Kay debated between a trade with Laura and a trade with the weaver and finally settled on one of the two.

2. Peter is not the potter.

3. Marge is not the one who does patchwork.

4. Joan is not the woodcarver or the weaver.

5. By the final trading arrangements, the potter traded two pieces of pottery, each with a different person; four of the six—Kay, Joan, the jewelry maker, and the woman who does patchwork—were involved in one each; and Olivia was involved in none. (*Note: All six exhibitors are mentioned in this clue.*)

The solution is on page 140.

	glass.	jewel.	patch.	potter	weaver	wood.
Joan						
Kay						
Laura						
Marge						
Olivia						
Peter						

THE
DELL BOOK
OF
LOGIC PROBLEMS

THE
DELL BOOK
OF
LOGIC PROBLEMS

Editor • Rosalind Moore

Senior Editor • Mary Ann Kennedy

A Dell Trade Paperback

A DELL TRADE PAPERBACK

Published by
Dell Publishing
a division of
Bantam Doubleday Dell Publishing Group, Inc.
1540 Broadway
New York, New York 10036

The trademark Dell® is registered in the U.S. Patent and Trademark Office.

ISBN: 0-440-51891-1

Printed in the United States of America

November 1984

30 29 28

KPP

A WORD ABOUT THIS BOOK

Logic Problems have become one of the most popular puzzles that Dell features in its many puzzle publications. And with good reason, we think, because Logic Problems are interesting, stimulating, challenging, and just plain fun to solve. People of all ages and all levels of solving skill can and do solve Logic Problems. The feeling of accomplishment you get after successfully completing an especially intricate Logic Problem is one of the true joys of puzzle solving.

Since Dell began presenting Logic Problems over 20 years ago, they have grown from occasional features, appearing a few times a year, to the more than 100 a year we currently publish. Yet, every day the mail brings pleas from Logic Problem addicts for more, more, more Logic Problems. Thus, this book, devoted exclusively to Logic Problems.

These Logic Problems have never been published before—they're all new. And the Logic Problem constructors whose puzzles appear herein are the cream of the crop. They are the same people who create the Logic Problems that are such an important part of the Dell puzzle publications. These puzzle constructors consistently create interesting, well-written, flawlessly reasoned puzzles that are wonderful entertainment. We are continually amazed at their talent and ingenuity. You will be too.

We hope and expect that you will enjoy the puzzles in this book, and we would very much like to know what you think about them. We invite your comments, either pro or con. All correspondence can be sent to the address below.

THE EDITORS
Dell Puzzle Publications
Dell Publishing
a division of
Bantam Doubleday Dell
Publishing Group, Inc.
1540 Broadway
New York, New York 10036

IN APPRECIATION

This book is the result of the efforts of many people. In addition to the talented constructors who created the Logic Problems in this book, to whom we are most grateful, we also especially want to thank Dodi Schultz, who is both Logic Problem constructor and trial solver. Her fine-tuning of all Dell's Logic Problems results in puzzles that approach perfection. We give special thanks to Kathleen Reineke, Frances Hendon, Margaret Doherty, Julie Spence, Theresa Atwood, Elyse Hilton, Linda Ostreicher, Emilia Klapper, Kate Rennie, Johanna Tani, Nancy Murray, Susan Reu, and Erica Rothstein, all of whom contributed their considerable expertise in helping to put this book together. Jack Morgan Ehn and Henry A. Kennedy, two non-Logic Problem solvers, deserve much credit for their patience and good humor in reviewing the How to Solve Logic Problems section as it was being written, pointing out what didn't seem to add up. We appreciate their unique contribution.

A book of Logic Problems was the dream of Kathleen Rafferty, for forty years the editor-in-chief of the Dell Puzzle Publications. We are particularly grateful to her for teaching us so much about puzzles. This book is lovingly dedicated to her.

The Editors

CONTENTS

EASY LOGIC PROBLEMS

MEDIUM LOGIC PROBLEMS

HARD LOGIC PROBLEMS

CHALLENGER LOGIC PROBLEMS

THE
DELL BOOK
OF
LOGIC PROBLEMS

HOW TO SOLVE LOGIC PROBLEMS

The 75 Logic Problems in this book are just that—problems (puzzles) based on logic—to which you need bring no specialized knowledge or extensive vocabulary. Instead, all you will need to solve Logic Problems is your common sense and a bit of reasoning power, plus a basic grasp of how to use the charts and/or other solving aids that are provided with almost all of the puzzles.

The Logic Problems in this book are classic deduction problems. In them you are usually asked to figure out how two or more sets of facts relate to each other—what first name belongs with which last name, for example. All of the facts you will need to solve each puzzle are always given.

Unless you really enjoy reading detailed instructions, by the way, we suggest that you now turn right to the first Logic Problem on page 27, read through both the introduction and the numbered clues, then take a pencil and start solving. If you should find yourself "stuck," you might want to read that puzzle's solution at the back of the book. See if you can follow the reasoning given. If you can, you're well on your way. Don't feel discouraged, though, if you still feel unsure about how Logic Problems are solved. The three examples that follow should help you get a grasp both on the reasoning processes involved in Logic Problems and also how you can use a Logic Problem chart to help you arrive at the puzzle's solution.

Printed below is a sample Logic Problem with its solving chart. Quickly read through both the introduction and the clues. Also notice that here, as in all the Logic Problems in this book, the last part of the introduction will tell you what facts you are to establish in solving the puzzle.

EXAMPLE #1

A young woman attending a party was introduced to four men in rather rapid succession and, as usual at such gatherings, their respective types of work were mentioned rather early in the conversation. Unfortunately, she was afflicted with a somewhat faulty memory. Half an hour later, she could remember only that she had met a Mr. Brown, a Mr. White, a Mr. Black, and a Mr. Green. She recalled that among them were a photographer, a grocer, a banker, and a singer, but she could not recall which was which. Her hostess, a fun-loving friend, refused to refresh her memory, but offered four clues. Happily, the young woman's logic was better than her memory, and she quickly paired each man with his profession. Can you? Here are the clues:

1. Mr. White approached the banker for a loan.

2. Mr. Brown had met the photographer when he hired him to take pictures of his wedding.

3. The singer and Mr. White are friends, but have never had business dealings.

4. Neither Mr. Black nor the singer had ever met Mr. Green before that evening.

	Black	Brown	Green	White
banker				
grocer				
photo.				
singer				

You know from the last part of the introduction what it is you are to determine—you are to match each man's last name with his profession. The chart has been set up to help you keep track of the information as you discover it. We suggest that you use an X in a box to indicate a definite impossibility and a • (dot) in a box to show an established fact.

Your first step is to enter X's into the chart for all of the obvious possibilities that you can see from information given in the clues. It is apparent from clue 1 that Mr. White is not the banker, so an X would be entered into the White/banker box. Clue 2 makes it clear that Mr. Brown is not the photographer, so another X in the Brown/photographer box can be entered. Clue 3 tells you that Mr. White is not the singer. And from clue 4 you can see that neither Mr. Black nor Mr. Green is the singer. Each of these impossibilities should also be indicated by X's in the chart. Once you have done so, your chart will look like this:

	Black	Brown	Green	White
banker				X
grocer				
photo.		X		
singer	X		X	X

Remembering that each X indicates that something is *not* a fact, note the row of boxes at the bottom—corresponding to which of the men is the singer. There are four possibilities, and you have X's for three of them. Therefore, Mr. Brown, the only one left, has to be the singer. Put a dot (•) in the singer/Brown box. Also, remember that if Mr. Brown is the singer, he is not the photographer (which we knew, we have an X); and he cannot be the grocer or the banker either. Thus, you would put X's in those boxes too. Your chart would now look like this:

	Black	Brown	Green	White
banker		X		X
grocer		X		
photo.		X		
singer	X	•	X	X

Now you seem to have a "hopeless" situation! You have used all the clues, and you have matched one man with his profession—but the additional X's entered in the chart do not enable you to make another match, since the possibilities have not been narrowed down sufficiently. What to do next?

Your next step is to reread the clues, at the same time considering the new information you have acquired: You know that Mr. Brown is the singer and that he has done business with the photographer (clue 2). But the singer has never done business with Mr. White (clue 3) or with Mr. Green (clue 4). And that means that neither Mr. White nor Mr. Green can possibly be the photographer. You can now place X's in those boxes in the chart. After you have done so, here is what you will have:

16

	Black	Brown	Green	White
banker		X		X
grocer		X		
photo.		X	X	X
singer	X	•	X	X

And you see that you do have more answers! The photographer must be Mr. Black, since there are X's in the boxes for the other names. Mr. White, also, must be the grocer, since there is an X in the other three boxes under his name. Once you have placed a dot to indicate that Mr. Black is the photographer and a dot to show that Mr. White is the grocer (always remembering to place X's in the other boxes in the row and column that contain the dot) your chart will look like this:

	Black	Brown	Green	White
banker	X	X		X
grocer	X	X	X	•
photo.	•	X	X	X
singer	X	•	X	X

You can see that you are left with one empty box, and this box corresponds to the remaining piece of information you have not yet determined—what Mr. Green's profession is and who the banker is. Obviously, the only possibility is that Mr. Green is the banker. And the Logic Problem is solved!

Most of the Logic Problems in this book will ask you to determine how more than two sets of facts are related to each other. You'll see, however, that the way of solving a more involved Logic Problem is just the same as Example #1—*if* you have a grasp of how to make the best use of the solving chart. The next example of a Logic Problem is presented in order to explain how to use a bigger chart. As before, read through the problem quickly, noting that the introduction tells you what facts you are to determine.

EXAMPLE #2

Andy, Chris, Noel, Randy, and Steve—one of whose last name is Morse—were recently hired as refreshment vendors at Memorial Stadium; each boy sells only one kind of fare. From the clues below, try to determine each boy's full name and the type of refreshment he sells.

1. Randy, whose last name is not Wiley, does not sell popcorn.

2. The Davis boy does not sell soda or candy.

3. The five boys are Noel, Randy, the Smith boy, the Coble boy, and the boy who sells ice cream.

4. Andy's last name is not Wiley or Coble. Neither Andy nor Coble is the boy who sells candy.

5. Neither the peanut vendor nor the ice cream vendor is named Steve or Davis.

17

	Coble	Davis	Morse	Smith	Wiley	candy	ice.	pean.	pop.	soda
Andy										
Chris										
Noel										
Randy										
Steve										
candy										
ice.										
pean.										
pop.										
soda										

In this puzzle you are going to match each boy's first name with his last name and establish which boy sells which type of refreshment. Note that the chart given below the clues is composed of three sets of boxes—one set corresponding to the first names and the last names; a second set of boxes to the right of the first set corresponding to the first names and the type of refreshment; and a third set, below the first set, corresponding to the type of refreshment and the last names. Notice, too, that these sets are separated from each other by heavier lines, so that it is easier to find the particular box you are looking for. You might not be sure why three sets of boxes are needed for this puzzle, but continue reading and you'll see!

As in Example #1, your first step is to enter into the boxes of the chart the impossibilities you are given in the clues. Keep in mind that you have many more boxes to be concerned with here. To minimize confusion in what follows, we will use the word ROW to indicate a set of boxes that goes horizontally (the Andy row, for example) and the word COLUMN will be used to indicate a set of boxes that goes vertically (the Coble column, for instance).

Clue 1 tells you that Randy's last name is not Wiley, and Randy does not sell popcorn. Thus, you will enter an X into the Randy/Wiley box and another X in the Randy/popcorn box of the Randy row. Clue 2 says that the Davis boy sells neither soda nor candy. Find the Davis column; then, going down that column, proceed to the Davis/soda box and put an X in it; then find the Davis/candy box in that same column and place an X in that box.

Clue 3 tells you a few things: It gives you all five of the boys, either by his first name (two of them), his last name (another two of them), or by what refreshment he sells (the remaining boy). You then know something about all five—one boy's first name is Noel, another's first name is Randy; a third boy has the last name Smith, a fourth boy has the last name Coble; and the fifth boy is the one who sells ice cream. Thus, all of these are different people—none of the facts given in this clue can match with any of the other facts given in the clue; it's impossible. So, in the chart you have a lot of X's that can be entered from the information in clue 3. Noel's last name is neither Smith nor Coble, so X's should be entered in the Noel/Smith, Noel/Coble boxes; nor can Noel be the ice cream seller, so put an X in the Noel/ice cream box also. Randy is neither Smith nor Coble, and Randy does not sell ice cream, so put the X's in the Randy/Smith, Randy/Coble, and Randy/ice cream boxes. And neither Smith nor Coble can be the ice cream seller, so go down the Smith column and the Coble column, find the box in each corresponding to ice cream, and enter an X in those two boxes.

Clue 4 tells you that Andy's last name is neither Wiley nor Coble. It also says that Andy does not sell candy and neither does the Coble boy. By now you probably know where to put the X's—in the Andy/Wiley box, the Andy/Coble box, the Andy/candy box, and in the box in the Coble column corresponding to candy. From clue 5 you learn that neither Steve nor Davis is the boy who sells either peanuts or ice cream. (One important point here—read clue 5 again, and note that this clue does *not* tell you whether or not Steve's last name is Davis; it tells you only that neither of the two boys who sell peanuts and ice cream has the first name Steve or the last name Davis.) Once you have entered all of the X's into the chart that you can at this point, your chart will look like this:

	Coble	Davis	Morse	Smith	Wiley	candy	ice.	pean.	pop.	soda
Andy	X				X	X				
Chris										
Noel	X		X				X			
Randy	X		X		X		X		X	
Steve							X	X		
candy	X	X								
ice.	X	X		X						
pean.		X								
pop.										
soda		X								

From this point on, we suggest that you fill in the above chart yourself as you read how the facts are established. If you will look at the Davis column, you will see that one fact is now known: You have X's in four of the refreshment boxes in the Davis column; therefore, the Davis boy is the one who sells popcorn. Put a dot in the Davis/popcorn box. Now, since it is Davis who sells popcorn, none of the other boys does, so you will put X's in all of the other boxes in that popcorn row.

Your next step will be to look up at the other set of refreshment boxes and see what first names already have an X in the popcorn column. Note that Randy has an X in the popcorn column (from clue 1). Thus, if you know that Randy does not sell popcorn, you now know that his last name is not Davis, since Davis is the popcorn seller. You can then put an X in the Randy/Davis box. After you've done this, you'll see that you now have four X's for Randy's last name. Randy has to be Morse, the only name left, so enter a dot in the Randy/Morse box; don't forget, too, to enter X's in the boxes of the Morse column that correspond to the first names of the other boys.

Now that you know Randy is Morse, you are ready to look at what you've already discovered about Randy and transfer that information to the Morse column—remember that since Randy is Morse, anything that you know about Randy you also know must be true of Morse, as they're the same person. You'll see that an X for Randy was entered from clue 3: Randy does not sell ice cream. Then Morse cannot be the ice cream seller either, so put an X in the Morse column to show that Morse doesn't sell ice cream.

Once the Morse/ice cream X is in place, note what you have established about the Wiley boy: His is the only last name left who can sell ice cream. Put the dot in the Wiley/ice cream box and enter X's in the Wiley column for all the other refreshments you now know Wiley does not sell. Your next step? As before, you are ready to determine what this new dot will tell you, so you will go up to the other set of refreshment boxes and see what you have established about the ice cream vendor. Clue 3 told you that Noel doesn't sell ice cream; from clue 5 you got that Steve doesn't sell ice cream either. Those two X's have already been entered in the chart. Now that you have established the Wiley boy as the ice cream seller, you know that his first name can't be either Noel or Steve because neither of those boys sells ice cream. Once you've put X's in the Noel/Wiley box and the Steve/Wiley box, you'll see that you know who Wiley is. Remember that clue 4 had already told you that Andy's last name is not Wiley, so you have an X in the Andy/Wiley box. With the new X's, do you see that Wiley's first name has to be Chris? And since Chris is Wiley, and Wiley sells ice cream, so, of course, does Chris. Thus, you can put a dot in the Chris/ice cream box. And don't forget to put X's in the Chris row for the other refreshments and also in the ice cream column for the other first names.

Notice that once Chris Wiley is entered in the chart, there are now four X's in the

Coble column, and Steve is the one who has to be the Coble boy. Put in the dot and then X's in the Steve row, and your chart looks like this:

	Coble	Davis	Morse	Smith	Wiley	candy	ice.	pean.	pop.	soda
Andy	X		X		X	X	X			
Chris	X	X	X	X	•	X	•	X	X	X
Noel	X		X	X	X		X			
Randy	X	X	•	X	X		X		X	
Steve	•	X	X	X	X			X	X	
candy	X	X			X					
ice.	X	X	X	X	•					
pean.		X			X					
pop.	X	•	X	X	X					
soda		X			X					

See that there are four X's in the Smith/first name column, so Smith's first name must be Andy. And Noel's last name is Davis, because he's the only one left. Remember—or look down the Davis row and see—that we already know Davis sells popcorn. Then Noel is the first name who should have a dot in the popcorn box. And, of course, there should be X's in all the other boxes of the Noel row and the popcorn column.

Now that you have completely established two sets of facts—which first name goes with which last name—you can use the two sets of refreshment boxes almost as one. That is, since you know each boy's first name and last name, anything you have determined about a first name will hold true for that boy's last name; and, naturally, the reverse is true: whatever you know about a last name must also be true of that boy's first name.

For example, look at the Coble column and note that you have already put X's in the candy, ice cream, and popcorn boxes. Go up to the other refreshment boxes and enter any X's for Steve that you know about Coble. After putting an X in the Steve/candy box, you'll see that you've determined that Steve sells soda—and, thus, the Coble column can now have a dot for soda too. As always, don't forget to enter X's where appropriate once you've entered a dot to indicate a determined fact. These X's are what will narrow down the remaining possibilities. Note that you already know that Andy does not sell candy. Once you've put an X to indicate that Smith (Andy's last name) doesn't sell candy, you'll see you have established that Morse sells candy—and, naturally, Randy does too, as he is Morse.

You're now left with two empty boxes, one in each set of refreshment boxes. By elimination, you can put a dot in each one. Andy sells peanuts; the Smith boy sells peanuts. As Andy is the Smith boy, these two dots match, you have determined all of the facts, and the Logic Problem is completely solved.

Many of the Logic Problems in this book will have charts that are set up much like the one in Example #2. They may be bigger, and the puzzle may involve matching up more sets of facts, but the method of solving the Logic Problem using the chart will be exactly the same: You will enter X's for any impossibilities you discover and dots whenever you have determined that something must be true. Don't forget to keep looking at the various sections of the chart to see if some X's or dots can be transferred from one section to another. If a particular puzzle does not exactly fit the pattern in one way or another, you will be aware of it while solving. Often, you will find that rereading the clues will help you if you seem to be "stuck." You may discover that you *do* know more facts than you thought you did.

Sometimes a Logic Problem has been created in such a way that the type of chart you learned about in Example #2 is not helpful in solving the problem. The puzzle itself is fine, but another kind of chart will better help you match up the facts and arrive at the correct solution. These charts may look different from each other, but the basic way of making use of them is the same. Example #3 is a puzzle using this type of solving chart.

EXAMPLE #3

It was her first visit home in ten years, and Louise wondered how she would manage to see her old friends and still take in the things she wanted to in the seven days she had to spend there. Her worry was needless, however, for when she got off the plane Sunday morning, there were her friends—Anna, Cora, Gert, Jane, Liz, and Mary—waiting to greet her with her seven-day visit all planned. The women knew that Louise wanted to revisit the restaurant where they always used to have lunch together, so Louise's vacation began that Sunday afternoon with a party. After that, each of the women had an entire day to spend with Louise, accompanying her to one of the following things: a ball game, concert, the theater, museum, zoo, and one day reserved for just shopping. From the clues below, find out who took Louise where and on what day.

1. Anna and the museum visitor and the woman whose day followed the zoo visitor were blondes; Gert and the concertgoer and the woman who spent Monday with Louise were brunettes. (*Note: All six women are mentioned in this clue.*)

2. Cora's day with Louise was not the visit that occurred the day immediately following Mary's day.

3. The six women visited with Louise in the following order: Jane was with Louise the day after the zoo visitor and four days before the museumgoer; Gert was with Louise the day after the theatergoer and the day before Mary.

4. Anna and the woman who took Louise shopping have the same color hair.

	Monday	Tuesday	Wednesday	Thursday	Friday	Saturday
friend						
activity						

As before (and always), read the entire puzzle through quickly. Note that here you are to determine which day, from Monday to Saturday, each woman spent with Louise and also what they did that day. The solving chart, often called a fill-in chart, is the best kind to use for this puzzle. You won't be entering X's and dots here; instead, you will be writing the facts into the chart as you determine them and also find out where they belong.

From clue 1 you can eliminate both Anna and Gert as the woman who took Louise to the museum and the concert. And neither of these activities took place on a Monday, nor did Anna or Gert spend Monday with Louise. You have discovered some things, but none of them can yet be entered into the chart. Most solvers find it useful to note these facts elsewhere, perhaps in the margin or on a piece of scratch paper, in their own particular kind of shorthand. Then when enough facts have been determined to begin writing them into the chart, you will already have them listed.

Do you see that clue 2 tells you Mary did not see Louise on Saturday? It's because the clue states that Cora's day was not the visit that occurred immediately following Mary's day, and thus, there had to be at least one visit after Mary's. You still don't have a definite fact to write into the chart. Don't lose heart, though, because . . .

21

. . . clue 3 will start to crack the puzzle! Note that this clue gives you the order of the visits. Since the days were Monday through Saturday, the only possible way for Jane to be with Louise the day after the zoo visitor and four days before the museumgoer is if the zoo visit took place on Monday, Jane was with Louise on Tuesday, and the museumgoer was with Louise on Saturday. These facts can now be written into the chart—Monday zoo, Tuesday Jane, Saturday museum. Three days have been accounted for. The last part of clue 3 gives you the other three days: with Wednesday, Thursday, and Friday still open, the theatergoer must be the Wednesday friend, Gert is the day after, or Thursday, and Mary saw Louise on Friday. These facts, too, should be written in the chart. Once you've done so, your chart will resemble this one:

	Monday	Tuesday	Wednesday	Thursday	Friday	Saturday
friend		Jane		Gert	Mary	
activity	zoo		theater			museum

Now go back to clue 1 and see what other facts you can establish. There are three blondes—Anna, the museum visitor, and the woman whose day followed the zoo visitor's. The chart shows you that this last woman was Jane. From clue 4 you learn that the woman who took Louise shopping and Anna have the same color hair—blonde. The woman who took Louise shopping is not Anna (they're two separate people), nor is she the museum visitor, so she must be the woman whose day followed the zoo visitor's, Jane. That fact can be written in the chart.

You can also, at this point, establish what day Anna spent with Louise. Since you know it's not Monday (clue 1) and Anna is not the museumgoer (also clue 1), the only day left for her is Wednesday, so Anna took Louise to the theater. Clue 2 tells you that Cora's day did not immediately follow Mary's, so Cora's day can't be Saturday, and must be Monday. By elimination, Liz (listed in the introduction) spent Saturday with Louise at the museum.

It may be helpful to make a note of the hair colors mentioned in clue 1, perhaps under the relevant columns in the chart. These hair colors can again be used at this point. We've now established the blondes as Anna, Jane, and Liz; the brunettes are Gert, the concertgoer, and Cora. The only possibility is that Mary is the concertgoer. Everything has now been determined except what Gert did, so, by elimination, Gert must have taken Louise to a ball game (from the introduction).

	Monday	Tuesday	Wednesday	Thursday	Friday	Saturday
friend	Cora	Jane	Anna	Gert	Mary	Liz
activity	zoo	shopping	theater	ball game	concert	museum
	bru	blo	blo	bru	bru	blo

Are all Logic Problems easy to solve? No, of course not. Many of the puzzles in this book are much more complicated than the three examples and should take a great deal more time and thought before you arrive at the solution. However, the techniques you use to solve the puzzles are essentially the same. All the information needed to solve will be given in the puzzle itself, either in the introduction or the clues. As you eliminate possibilities, you will narrow down the choices until, finally, you can establish a certainty. That certainty will usually help narrow down the possibilities in another set of facts. Once you have determined something, you will probably need to return to the clues and reread them, keeping in mind what facts you have now established. Suddenly a sentence in the clues may well tell you something you could not have determined before, thus narrowing down the choices still further. Eventually you will have determined everything, and the Logic Problem will be solved.

The puzzles in this book are mostly arranged in increasing order of difficulty—the first few are rather easy to solve, then the puzzles get more difficult as you continue through the book. The final 15 puzzles are especially challenging. If you are new to Logic Problems, we suggest that you start with the first puzzles, progressing through the book as you get more expert at solving.

EASY LOGIC PROBLEMS

1 THE DANCE CONTEST

by Randall L. Whipkey

The Cozy Inn dance contest is an annual event in which couples dance their specialties in open competition for five prizes of $50 for first, $40 for second, $30 for third, $20 for fourth, and $10 for fifth. At this year's event, five men—Roger, Stan, Thad, Victor, and Warren—and their partners—(in no particular order) Harriet, Inez, Jane, Karen, and Linda—won the prizes by dancing (at random) a fox trot, jitterbug, polka, tango, and waltz. From the clues below, can you determine the man and woman who made up each couple, each couple's dance specialty, and the prize each won?

1. Jane and her partner, and the couple that won $10, and the couple that jitterbugged were all in their first contest, while the other two couples—Victor and his partner and the couple who tangoed—were entered in their second. (*Note: All five couples are mentioned.*)

2. Three couples—Warren and his partner, Harriet and her partner, and the couple who won $30—all danced on local television as a result of the Cozy Inn contest; neither the couple who did the tango nor Karen and her partner were invited to appear on television. (*Note: All five are mentioned.*)

3. Victor and his partner, Karen and her partner, and the contestants who won $20 are all married couples.

4. The five prizes were awarded as follows: first, to Stan and his partner; second, to the couple who did the fox trot; third, to Linda and her partner; fourth, to the couple who did the polka; fifth, to Thad and his partner.

The solution is on page 139.

	Harriet	Inez	Jane	Karen	Linda	fox	jitter.	polka	tango	waltz	$50	$40	$30	$20	$10
Roger															
Stan															
Thad															
Victor															
Warren															
$50															
$40															
$30															
$20															
$10															
fox															
jitter.															
polka															
tango															
waltz															

2 LAS VEGAS WEEKEND

by Margaret Ruff

Four couples from Los Angeles, the Blums, Browns, Steels, and Joneses, went to Las Vegas for the weekend. Two couples stayed at the Star Hotel, one at the Moon Hotel, and one stayed at the Sun Hotel. Saturday night, each couple went to a dinner show, but only one couple saw the show at the hotel where they were staying. The shows they saw were at the Star Hotel, the Moon Hotel, the Hill, and Nero's Castle. The men's names were Charles, Eric, John, and Max, the women's were Grace, Irene, Mae, and Sarah. From the clues below, determine the full names of each couple, at which hotel each stayed, and which dinner show each saw.

1. The couple who stayed at the Moon saw the Nero's Castle show.

2. Max Blum liked the dancing he saw at the Star show.

3. Mae would not leave her hotel for a show.

4. Sarah Steel went to the Hill.

5. Eric always stays at the Sun when he's in town.

6. Charles and Grace Brown stayed at the Star.

The solution is on page 139.

		Charles	Eric	John	Max	Grace	Irene	Mae	Sarah	hotel Star	Star	Moon	Sun	show Nero's	Star	Hill	Moon
	Blum																
	Brown																
	Steel																
	Jones																
show	Nero's																
	Star																
	Hill																
	Moon																
hotel	Star																
	Star																
	Moon																
	Sun																
	Grace																
	Irene																
	Mae																
	Sarah																

28

3 THE GOLDEN-AGERS

by Fred H. Dale

The Golden Age Retirement Home has a remarkable group of five women—one is named Louise—who are more than 90 years of age. No two are the same age, and none has reached 100 (all ages are considered to be in whole numbers). With the aid of the following clues, you should be able to decide the full name and age of each.

1. Jenny's age is halfway between Mrs. Bowen's and Mrs. Jones's.

2. Sarah is older than Mrs. Jones, but younger than Jenny.

3. All the women's ages are in even numbers, except Mrs. Wall's.

4. Susan is neither the oldest nor the youngest.

5. Mrs. King is as much older than Anna as Mrs. Walker is older than Mrs. King.

We've left empty boxes in the ages row and column for you to fill them in when you determine what they are.

The solution is on page 139.

	Anna	Jenny	Louise	Sarah	Susan	ages				
Bowen										
Jones										
King										
Walker										
Wall										
a g e s										

29

4 FOOTBALL GAME WATCHERS

by Margaret Shoop

Four friends, including Mike, gathered at Mike's home on a Sunday afternoon to watch a football game on television between the Washington Warriors and the New York Braves. From the clues that follow, can you determine each fan's last name (one is Blakely) and occupation (one is a statistician)?

1. Two of Mike's guests were Donna and the building contractor.

2. Hugh, whose last name isn't Horner, is a loyal Braves fan.

3. Donna isn't the dentist.

4. Jenkins, an avid Warrior fan, went home before the game was over, following an apparently conclusive Braves touchdown late in the fourth quarter, which put the Braves in the lead.

5. Jean and Anderson were both delighted to watch the Warriors win the game with a touchdown in the final seconds.

6. The programmer was the last person to go home.

7. Horner isn't the building contractor.

The solution is on page 140.

The solution is on page 140.

	Anderson	Blakely	Horner	Jenkins	bldg. cont.	dentist	program.	statis.
Mike								
Donna								
Hugh								
Jean								
bldg. cont.								
dentist								
program.								
statis.								

7 THE VACATIONERS

by Fred H. Dale

The Harrisons and four other couples spent their vacations in different places (one visited Canada) and in different fashions last year. One couple stayed at a campground, another backpacked, and a third went on a cruise. Can you decide from the following clues where each couple went and the way they spent their vacation? *Note:* Vans and pickup campers are considered to be recreational vehicles.

1. Neither the Joneses—who did not visit Alaska—nor the couple who visited Yellowstone National Park traveled in recreational vehicles.

2. Neither the couple who traveled in a pickup camper nor the one who traveled in a van visited Alaska.

3. The Aldriches are not the couple who spent their vacation in the Oregon mountains, nor did they travel by pickup camper.

4. The couple who traveled in a van did not visit New England; the couple who traveled in a pickup camper did not visit Oregon.

5. The Johnsons, who did not go backpacking, did not travel in a van or camper and did not visit Alaska.

6. The Wilsons did not travel by recreational vehicle.

7. Neither the couple who went to Oregon nor the one who visited Yellowstone took a cruise; the backpackers did not go to Yellowstone.

The solution is on page 140.

	Alaska	Canada	New Eng.	Oregon	Yellow.	camping	backpack	cruise	van	pickup
Aldrich										
Harrison										
Johnson										
Jones										
Wilson										
camp										
backpack										
cr										
v										
p										

8 THE DEFUNCT-CAR CLUB

by Randall L. Whipkey

The Cozy Valley Defunct-Car Club is a new organization whose members each own an automobile that has gone out of production. The five club members each own a different make of car—either a Nike, Hydra, Kratos, Sibyl, or Pegasus—and each car is of a different model year—either '47, '49, '51, '53, or '55. From the following clues, can you determine each member's first name—either Larry, Mark, Harry, James, or George— and last name—which might be Andrews, Brooks, Conway, Davis, or East—as well as the make of car he owns and the year it was made?

1. The three oldest cars are owned by George and Mr. Brooks and James, although not necessarily in that order.

2. The Nike is older than Mark's defunct car.

3. Mr. Conway's car is older than the Kratos.

4. Harry's auto is two years older than the Pegasus.

5. Mr. Andrews's auto is older than either the Sibyl or Mr. Davis's model.

6. The Kratos is two years older than George's auto and four years older than the Nike.

The solution is on page 141.

The solution is on page 141.

	Andrews	Brooks	Conway	Davis	East	Hydra	Kratos	Nike	Pegasus	Sibyl	'47	'49	'51	'53	'55
George															
Harry															
James															
Larry															
Mark															
'47															
'49															
'51															
'53															
'55															
Hydra															
Kratos															
Nike															
Pegasus															
Sibyl															

8 THE DEFUNCT-CAR CLUB

by Randall L. Whipkey

The Cozy Valley Defunct-Car Club is a new organization whose members each own an automobile that has gone out of production. The five club members each own a different make of car—either a Nike, Hydra, Kratos, Sibyl, or Pegasus—and each car is of a different model year—either '47, '49, '51, '53, or '55. From the following clues, can you determine each member's first name—either Larry, Mark, Harry, James, or George— and last name—which might be Andrews, Brooks, Conway, Davis, or East—as well as the make of car he owns and the year it was made?

1. The three oldest cars are owned by George and Mr. Brooks and James, although not necessarily in that order.

2. The Nike is older than Mark's defunct car.

3. Mr. Conway's car is older than the Kratos.

4. Harry's auto is two years older than the Pegasus.

5. Mr. Andrews's auto is older than either the Sibyl or Mr. Davis's model.

6. The Kratos is two years older than George's auto and four years older than the Nike.

The solution is on page 141.

	Andrews	Brooks	Conway	Davis	East	Hydra	Kratos	Nike	Pegasus	Sibyl	'47	'49	'51	'53	'55
George															
Harry															
James															
Larry															
Mark															
'47															
'49															
'51															
'53															
'55															
Hydra															
Kratos															
Nike															
Pegasus															
Sibyl															

7 THE VACATIONERS

by Fred H. Dale

The Harrisons and four other couples spent their vacations in different places (one visited Canada) and in different fashions last year. One couple stayed at a campground, another backpacked, and a third went on a cruise. Can you decide from the following clues where each couple went and the way they spent their vacation? *Note:* Vans and pickup campers are considered to be recreational vehicles.

1. Neither the Joneses—who did not visit Alaska—nor the couple who visited Yellowstone National Park traveled in recreational vehicles.

2. Neither the couple who traveled in a pickup camper nor the one who traveled in a van visited Alaska.

3. The Aldriches are not the couple who spent their vacation in the Oregon mountains, nor did they travel by pickup camper.

4. The couple who traveled in a van did not visit New England; the couple who traveled in a pickup camper did not visit Oregon.

5. The Johnsons, who did not go backpacking, did not travel in a van or camper and did not visit Alaska.

6. The Wilsons did not travel by recreational vehicle.

7. Neither the couple who went to Oregon nor the one who visited Yellowstone took a cruise; the backpackers did not go to Yellowstone.

The solution is on page 140.

	Alaska	Canada	New Eng.	Oregon	Yellow.	camping	backpack	cruise	van	pickup
Aldrich										
Harrison										
Johnson										
Jones										
Wilson										
camping										
backpack										
cruise										
van										
pickup										

9 LEARNING A TRADE

by Evelyn B. Rosenthal

Mr. Green and two other artisans work in different fields. Each has a son whom he has trained in his own work, but who expressed a desire to learn something of the other two crafts as well. So last summer each boy worked as an apprentice for one of the other two men in July and for the second in August (each man had only one apprentice at a time). From the following clues, can you find the full names of all six (one is Bud), each father's trade, and who was apprenticed to whom each month?

1. Ted worked for the electrician in July and for Abe in August.

2. Dan, whose last name is not Brown, did not work for the mechanic during the summer.

3. Mr. White is not the carpenter, nor is his first name Abe.

4. The boy named Hal is not the one who worked for Joe in August.

We did not find a chart to be helpful in solving this puzzle. We suggest you use the space below to write down the facts as you establish them.

The solution is on page 141.

10 THE WILDLIFE WALK

by W. H. Organ

Just north of the village of Maple Hollow, there are five farm properties extending in a northerly direction along the east side of a country road; a small stream called Bear Creek meanders in a northerly direction through the three southernmost of the five, then veers sharply eastward without touching the other two properties. Last summer, the nature counselor at Maple Hollow Day Camp obtained permission from the Cranes and the other four owners to take a group of youngsters on a hike going in a northerly direction through the wooded areas of the properties in order to observe the wildlife.

During the hike, Carl and the other four children who participated each spotted a different animal and each, as it happens, was spotted on a different property. From the following clues, can you give the relative locations of the five farms, who owns which, and tell who spotted what where? (One of the animals sighted was a squirrel.)

1. The hike did not start or finish on the Moore farm, and the rabbit was not sighted on the Moore's property.

2. Jill spotted her animal by an oak tree growing alongside Bear Creek; it was not the deer.

3. Daisy sighted the first animal.

4. The Brooks farm, which is not where Will spotted an animal, is north of at least one of the others but south of the one where a fox was seen running away from a red barn.

5. The deer was not the first animal sighted.

6. Ellen spotted her animal on the Arden farm; it was the next animal to be sighted after the skunk.

7. Bear Creek runs through the Noble farm.

8. One of the Brooks's two immediate neighbors owns the only one of the five farms with a red barn.

9. One of the boys spotted the skunk as it was drinking from Bear Creek.

We found this diagram of the five farms to be most helpful in solving this puzzle.

The solution is on page 141.

owner   hiker   animal

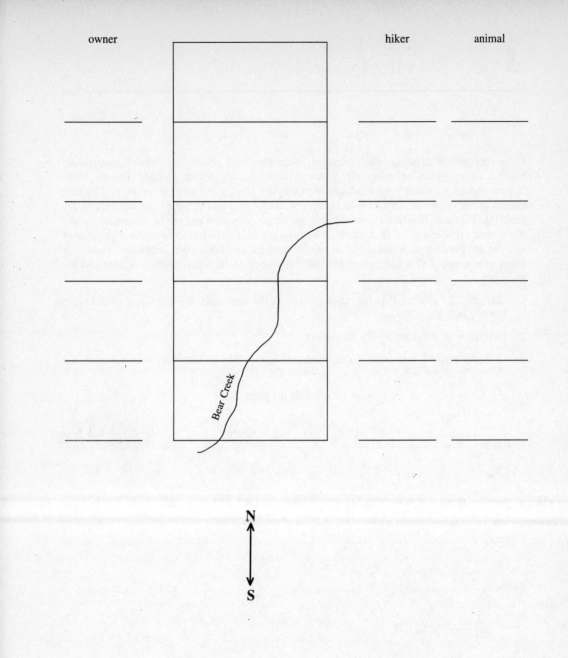

Bear Creek

N
↑
↓
S

37

11 NIGHT ON THE TOWN

by Frank A. Bauckman

Four corporation officers, the President, Vice-President, Secretary, and Treasurer are named, in no particular order, Mr. Black, Mr. White, Mr. Gold, and Mr. Brown. Each has an unmarried sister who works as secretary for one of the other three men. The first names of the men are Robert, Edwin, Henry, and Alvin and those of the secretaries are Roberta, Edwina, Henrietta, and Alvina, all in no particular order. No secretary works for a man with a similar first name. The men recently decided to take their secretaries out for an evening at a supper club. Each man escorted his own secretary. From the clues given, see if you can determine the full names of each corporation officer and his secretary.

1. Mr. Black escorted Edwina; they arrived at the club after the President, but before Henry and Miss Brown.

2. Alvina was escorted by the Treasurer.

3. Edwina arrived just after Robert and just before Mr. White; she was not with the Vice-President, who arrived second with Edwin's sister.

The solution is on page 142.

with secretary

President _____ _____ _____ _____

Vice-President _____ _____ _____ _____

Secretary _____ _____ _____ _____

Treasurer _____ _____ _____ _____

12 THE NEIGHBORHOOD CHILDREN

by Virginia C. McCarthy

Five children, all of different ages ranging from three to seven, live on the same block on Elm Street. From the following clues, can you find the full names and ages of the five children?

1. Every Saturday afternoon, Mrs. Gray goes to work and leaves her children with Mrs. White, whose daughter is younger than Mrs. Gray's children.

2. Tina is older than Larry and younger than the Green child.

3. The Brown girl is two years older than Lisa.

4. Rita's mother, who is sometimes home on Saturday afternoons, occasionally takes care of Gary while his mother goes shopping for the afternoon.

Note from clue 1 that there are two Gray children. Thus, the Gray column will have two dots in it to indicate the two children's first names.

The solution is on page 142.

	Brown	Gray	Green	White	ages 3	4	5	6	7
Gary									
Larry									
Lisa									
Rita									
Tina									
ages 3				
4				
5				
6				
7				

MEDIUM LOGIC PROBLEMS

13 HURRICANE IWA

by W. H. Organ

Iwa is the Hawaiian name for the great frigate bird. It is also the name that was given to one of their most destructive hurricanes. At one location overlooking the hard-hit south coast of one of the islands, six homes, including that of the Freemans, stood up well under the violent winds of Iwa. At each home, however, two trees were lost to the storm; each family lost a mango or a palm, plus an avocado, a papaya, or a plumeria. Interestingly, each family's anemometer registered a different maximum wind velocity during the storm. From the following clues, can you determine the trees each family lost and the highest wind speed (in whole miles per hour) registered by each of their anemometers?

1. Each family lost a different combination of trees.

2. The Deans did not own an avocado tree.

3. The Ambroses' palm tree fell before either of the avocado trees in their neighbors' yards. Their anemometer registered 103, the highest of the six homes.

4. The Baldwins did not own a palm tree. Their anemometer registered 98, which was lower than any of the others.

5. The Elmores' palm tree fell before their plumeria.

6. The Cases' anemometer read higher than the Elmores' but lower than the Deans'.

7. The home where the anemometer registered 99 lost a mango tree and a papaya.

Note from the puzzle's introduction that each family lost either a mango or a palm, as well as one other tree. Keep in mind as you fill in the chart, therefore, that you will not be able to automatically put X's in all rows or columns once you've determined a fact

The solution is on page 143.

	mango	palm	avocado	papaya	plumeria	wind					
Ambrose											
Baldwin											
Case				·							
Dean											
Elmore											
Freeman											
wind											

14 THE HAPPY DIETERS

by Carol Johnson

At the last meeting of the ''Dieting Is Easier Together'' (D.I.E.T.) club Mrs. Oliver and three of her friends discovered they had lost a total of exactly 100 pounds. They could hardly wait to tell their husbands, who had just enjoyed a filling dinner and were waiting for them in a nearby restaurant. Over coffee (black, of course) the four couples discussed the women's weight losses. From the clues below, try to determine each couple's full name, and how much weight each wife lost.

1. Fran, who lost 6 pounds more than one of the other women, lost 8 pounds less than Art's wife.

2. Bill congratulated Mrs. Paulson for losing 30 pounds, wondering if his wife would ever lose that much.

3. Gloria told her brother-in-law, Dave, that she lost more than both Eva and Mrs. Miller, but not as much as Mrs. Nelson.

4. Helen lost 10 pounds more than Clyde's wife.

The solution is on page 143.

	Art	Bill	Clyde	Dave	Miller	Nelson	Oliver	Paulson	lbs. lost			
Eva												
Fran												
Gloria												
Helen												
lbs. lost												
Miller												
Nelson												
Oliver												
Paulson												

15 A WHO-DONE-IT-FIRST MYSTERY

by M. J. Arterberry

The senior class play this year was an original murder mystery in which the victim was "done in" five different ways by five different villains: Bela Lugosi, Boris Karloff, Lon Chaney, Peter Lorre, and Sydney Greenstreet. The first villain to reach him actually killed the victim, but left him sitting up in such a position that he did not appear dead, so the subsequent villain visitors each went ahead with his murderous act also. As a spectator, see if you can solve this case from the following clues. Match each villain with his role in the play (forger, gangster, maniac, smuggler, or spy), the method he used to effect the killing, and the order in which he reached the victim.

1. The person with the poison dart got to the victim before Peter Lorre did, but the dart did not kill the victim.

2. Lon Chaney arrived before the strangler, but the man using electric shock had already been there.

3. The gangster did his dirty work before the spy, who in turn arrived before the man with the gun, who was next to last in his efforts.

4. Boris Karloff got to the victim before Sydney Greenstreet did, but the strangler had already been there.

5. Lon Chaney reached the victim before the maniac, as well as before the wielder of the dagger.

6. The smuggler said next time he would try using a dagger instead of the method he employed this time.

7. Boris Karloff vowed that the maniac would never beat him to the "kill" again.

The solution is on page 143.

	villain	role	method
1st	_____	_____	_____
2nd	_____	_____	_____
3rd	_____	_____	_____
4th	_____	_____	_____
5th	_____	_____	_____

16

THE IVY LEAGUERS

by Haydon Calhoun

Five undergraduates named Atkins, Ford, Inman, Jacobs, and Massey are honor students at Ivy League schools, namely, but not necessarily respectively, Cornell, Dartmouth, Harvard, Princeton, and Yale. Each, as it happens, is also an outstanding athlete—either a boxer, an equestrian, a gymnast, a sprinter, or a weight lifter (again, not necessarily respectively). From the clues below, can you determine each man's first name (from among Kip, Nat, Russ, Ted, and Vic), last name, his school, and the sport in which he competes?

1. The Cornell man is studying law, while Ford is a science major; Nat and Inman and the Princeton man are all business majors.

2. Kip and Atkins are seniors, whereas Russ and Ford are juniors, the boxer a sophomore.

3. Inman, whose first name is not Russ, is not the Harvard sprinter.

4. Counting high school participation, both Vic and the sprinter have been competing in amateur meets for five years, the gymnast four, Ford three, and the weight lifter two.

5. Inman is not the gymnast and does not attend Dartmouth.

6. Jacobs is not the Princeton boxer.

The solution is on page 144.

	Kip	Nat	Russ	Ted	Vic	Cor.	Dart.	Har.	Prin.	Yale	boxer	equest.	gym.	sprin.	weight.
Atkins															
Ford															
Inman															
Jacobs															
Massey															
boxer															
equest.															
gym.															
sprin.															
weight.															
Cor.															
Dart.															
Har.															
Prin.															
Yale															

17 THE PIZZA PARLOR

by Randall L. Whipkey

For an after-the-movie snack, five couples—the Colliers, Leonards, Morgans, Nelsons, and Walkers—decided to stop at Lou's Pizza Parlor. Each of the couples satisfied their taste by ordering a different style of pizza—(in no particular order) anchovy, cheese, mushroom, pepperoni, or sausage, and their hunger by ordering a different size pizza—variously, 20″, 18″, 16″, 14″, or 12″ in diameter. When their checks came, each couple owed a different amount of money for their pizza, variously $3.50, $3.00, $2.75, $2.25, or $2.00. From the clues below, can you deduce the style and size of pizza each couple ordered and its price? (*Note: Prices at Lou's are not dependent on size alone!*)

1. The pizza the Morgans ordered cost more than $2.00.

2. The 16″ pizza cost 50¢ less than the mushroom pizza, and the mushroom pizza cost less than the sausage pizza.

3. The pizza the Colliers bought cost more than the 18″ pizza.

4. The Leonards' pizza cost 75¢ more than the 14″ pizza.

5. The anchovy pizza cost 75¢ more than the 12″ pizza.

6. The Walkers' pizza cost 75¢ more than the pepperoni pizza, which wasn't the pizza with the lowest price.

The solution is on page 144.

	anchovy	cheese	mushroom	pepperoni	sausage	20″	18″	16″	14″	12″	$3.50	$3.00	$2.75	$2.25	$2.00
Colliers															
Leonards															
Morgans															
Nelsons															
Walkers															
$3.50															
$3.00															
$2.75															
$2.25															
$2.00															
20″															
18″															
16″															
14″															
12″															

18 LETTERS TO THE EDITOR

by Jean M. Hannagan

Among a certain puzzle magazine editor's mail one day were five letters from fans. All five were from different states, including Louisiana and Oregon, and all five expressed enthusiasm for the magazine, but each cited a different favorite feature and, interestingly, all five writers have different careers. From the following clues, and the facts that one letter was from an engineer, one from a woman named Iris, and one from a solver named Rogers, can you determine the full name, favorite puzzle, and occupation of each solver, and where each lives? *Note to non–U.S. solvers:* New Jersey and Pennsylvania are in the Northeast; California and Oregon are in the West; Louisiana is in the South.

1. Kurt lives in a northeastern state; both the crossword fan and solver Vaughn, whose first name is not Henry, live in the western part of the country.

2. The solver from Pennsylvania (who is not the artist) and Mrs. Smith have both been solving puzzles for many years.

3. The last name of the interior decorator, who lives in New Jersey, is not Thorpe.

4. The English teacher's favorites are the diagramless puzzles.

5. Neither the Californian nor the quiz fan is named George; and neither the Californian nor the quiz fan is the accountant.

6. Kurt and Joan have just recently discovered the fun of puzzle solving; their favorites are the cryptograms and the mazes (not necessarily in that order).

7. Miss Underwood is an enthusiastic solver but has never tried doing cryptograms.

Because of the unusually large number of facts in this puzzle, we found it necessary to divide the chart into two parts. However, these charts are used in the normal way.

The solution is on page 144.

	George	Henry	Iris	Joan	Kurt	Cal.	La.	N.J.	Ore.	Pa.	acc't.	artist	engineer	teach.	int. dec.
Rogers															
Smith															
Thorpe															
Underwood															
Vaughn															
acc't.															
artist															
engineer															
teach.															
int. dec.															
Cal.															
La.															
N.J.															
Ore.															
Pa.															

	crosswd.	crypt.	diag.	maze	quiz
George					
Henry					
Iris					
Joan					
Kurt					
Rogers					
Smith					
Thorpe					
Underwood					
Vaughn					
acc't.					
artist					
engineer					
teach.					
int. dec.					
Cal.					
La.					
N.J.					
Ore.					
Pa.					

19 THE MODELS CLUB

by Karen J. Allen

Among recent recruits to Center City's Models Club, which is composed of taller-than-average women, are Connie, Donna, Marie, Mildred, and Tracy, whose last names are—in one order or another—Davis, Denny, Hastings, Keeshan, and Williams. Your task is to discover, from the clues below, each woman's full name, the relative ages of the five, and each woman's exact height—one is 5'9", two are 5'10", one is 5'11", and the other is 6'.

1. The oldest, who is not Ms. Davis, is taller than Tracy but shorter than Connie or Mildred.

2. Ms. Keeshan, who is taller than Connie, is also older than both Connie and Donna.

3. Marie's and Donna's last names both begin with the same letter.

4. Tracy is older than Ms. Williams and at least one of the other women.

5. Ms. Davis is not the youngest.

6. The tallest woman is younger than the shortest.

The solution is on page 145.

	Connie	Donna	Marie	Mildred	Tracy	5'9"	5'10"	5'10"	5'11"	6'	young-est				old-est
Davis															
Denny															
Hastings															
Keeshan															
Williams															
youngest															
oldest															
5'9"															
5'10"															
5'10"															
5'11"															
6'															

20 PRESIDENTIAL NAMES

by W. H. Organ

The Brents and the Bonds (who have just moved in next door to the Brents) have discovered they have something in common: each of their children has a middle name that is the surname of a former U.S. president; one is Monroe. All the middle names are different. From the following clues, can you determine the full names of all the youngsters in both families and what high school class each is in?

1.   John's sister's middle name is not Adams.

2.   James and one of the boys who has just moved in next door to him are juniors in high school.

3.   Edward, whose middle name is Wilson, is not related to Alice.

4.   Brendan, who is not the one whose middle name is Grant, is a high-school senior.

5.   One of the two sophomores' middle names is Garfield; the other's is Adams.

6.   Peter is a high school freshman.

7.   One of the juniors' middle names is Lincoln.

8.   James has just one brother.

The solution is on page 145.

	Alice	Brendan	Edward	James	John	Peter	Bond	Brent	class					
Adams														
Garfield														
Grant														
Lincoln														
Monroe														
Wilson														
class														
Bond														
Brent														

21 ZODIAC FAMILY TREE

by M. J. Arterberry

Mr. and Mrs. Strange, their five daughters and their five sons-in-law were each born under a different sign of the zodiac. Combining their interests in astrology and creative art, the Stranges constructed a metal family tree for the amateur art contest at the county fair. The base of the tree consisted of stylized supports representing Aquarius, Mr. Strange's birth sign, and Virgo, Mrs. Strange's sign. From the base rose a branch supporting five plaques. The plaques were painted with the zodiacal signs of a daughter and her husband beside each other. The signs are: Aries, Taurus, Gemini, Moon Children, Leo, Libra, Scorpio, Sagittarius, Capricorn, and Pisces.

If the oldest daughter's plaque stands highest, with the others lower according to age, try to determine the order of the five daughters by name and the signs that represent each daughter–husband combination from these clues.

1. The Libra plaque, which is not the highest, is just above Ann's.

2. Although Mary's plaque is not the highest, it is higher than both the one representing Moon Children and Olga's plaque.

3. Capricorn is between Trudy's plaque and the Gemini plaque.

4. Trudy's plaque isn't as high as the Aries one, but four, including the two just mentioned, the Sagittarius plaque, and Rosie's plaque, are higher than Leo.

5. Pisces is just below Taurus on the plaques.

6. Two plaques separate Mary's plaque from the one with Gemini on it.

The "family tree" diagram is what we used to solve this Logic Problem.

The solution is on page 145.

daughter   signs

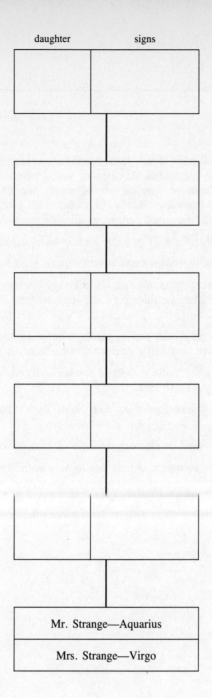

Mr. Strange—Aquarius

Mrs. Strange—Virgo

22 FAMILY FUN

by Joanne Horton

Mrs. Williams's seven children—Fred, Jack, Joan, Laura, Mary, Matt, and Ruth—are a delight to her because they are all bright, outgoing young people and the house is always bustling with activity. None is married yet, although one of the two older girls is engaged to Russ, and the rest all go steady. From the clues given below, see if you can give the ages, favored activities, and current steadies of the Williams children.

1. The two oldest daughters are 21 and 23. Jack is older than Mary.

2. The 17-year-old is on the swim team at school, and aims for the Olympics.

3. When Bill and Bruce come to call on their girlfriends, they usually also go downstairs to admire Matt's guinea pigs and see how the 12-year-old's model trains are progressing.

4. The 16-year-old, a high school junior, paints in her spare time; the 13-year-old is in her third year of ballet, and Bill's girlfriend has a fantastic stamp collection.

5. Joan, who loves to knit, made a sweater for her older sister last year; now she is trying to teach Becky how to knit.

6. Jim, who is a high school freshman, too, holds Ruth's hand when he walks her home from school.

7. The youngest boy is sweet on Barbara, and the 14-year-old calls Donna every night.

Because of the size of the solving chart, it had to be divided in two. Use as a regular chart, however.

The solution is on page 146.

	swim	guinea pig	train	paint	ballet	stamp	knit	ages					
Fred													
Jack													
Joan													
Laura													
Mary													
Matt													
Ruth													
Barb.													
Becky													
Bill													
Bruce													
Donna													
Jim													
Russ													

ages

	Barb.	Becky	Bill	Bruce	Donna	Jim	Russ
Fred							
Jack							
Joan							
Laura							
Mary							
Matt							
Ruth							

23 METROPOLITAN EXECUTIVES

by Diane C. Baldwin

Weekday mornings, Smith and three other executives travel to work by bus, and each of their offices is on a different floor of the five-story Metropolitan Building. This beautiful square structure has an entrance in the center of each of its sides (each side directly faces a compass point) and bus stops at each of its corners. From the following clues, can you identify each of the four arriving executives by his floor number, the entrance he uses (each uses a different entrance, and each uses one of the two that are nearest his stop), and his bus stop location?

1. From his own bus stop, Brown can see a second bus stop, which Block uses, and still another bus stop, which the first-floor and the fourth-floor executives use.

2. The executive who walks east to the south entrance works on the floor directly above Lane.

3. There is a floor between Block and the executive above who uses the west entrance, but Block is directly above the floor of one of the other executives.

4. Lane doesn't work on the first floor.

The solution is on page 146.

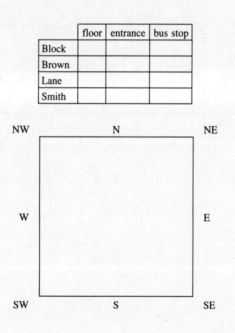

	floor	entrance	bus stop
Block			
Brown			
Lane			
Smith			

24 THE AMBASSADORS

by Lois Bohnsack

Mssrs. Carter, Kreech, Morley, Stamey, and Vance were recently appointed as ambassadors to five European nations. Each appointee, as it happens, is fluent in the language of precisely one of these countries, but none has been appointed to the country where he speaks the native language, so each is presently taking an intensive course in the language of the country in which he will serve. From the clues below, determine each man's first name, the language he spoke fluently before his appointment, and the country in which he will serve.

1. Neither Peter, Erwin, nor Mr. Kreech will be ambassador to Spain.

2. Neither Howard nor the ambassador to Italy can speak Russian or German.

3. Neither the man who speaks Italian nor Mr. Vance will be living in France.

4. Mr. Stamey is originally from New York. Mr. Kreech and the man who speaks Spanish are both from California. Randy and the ambassador to Italy are both from Illinois. (*Note: all five men are mentioned.*)

5. The five ambassadors are: Howard, Mr. Carter, Alan, the ambassador to the U.S.S.R., and the man who speaks Italian.

6. Peter does not speak German.

The solution is on page 147.

	A	F	H	P	R	Fr.	Ger.	It.	Russ.	Span.	France	Germany	Italy	USSR	Spain
Carter															
Kreech															
Morley															
Stamey															
Vance															
France																
Germany																
Italy																
USSR																
Spain																
Fr.																
Ger.																
It.																
Russ.																
Span.																

25 THE TEMPS

by Randall L. Whipkey

The Temps is an employment agency specializing in temporary office help. Last week, Carol and four other women received assignments, one woman at a law firm. Each of the five assignments was for a different number of days, from one to five. From the clues below, can you determine each woman's full name, the type of client who hired her, and the number of days for which she was engaged?

1. Andrea was hired for one more day than Ms. Wilson, who was hired for one more day than the woman who worked for the accountants.

2. Ms. Young, whose first name isn't Andrea, wasn't hired by the stockbrokers.

3. Betsy, who didn't work for the accountants, isn't Ms. Valley.

4. Ellen was hired for two more days than Ms. Young.

5. Ms. Wilson wasn't the one hired by the physicians.

6. Ms. Thomas was hired for two more days than the woman who worked for the stockbrokers, who was not Ms. Stevens.

7. Ellen wasn't the woman hired by the stockbrokers.

8. Denise isn't Ms. Thomas.

9. Ms. Stevens didn't work for either the physicians or the dentists.

The solution is on page 147.

The solution is on page 147.

	Andrea	Betsy	Carol	Denise	Ellen	acc't.	dent.	law.	phys.	stock.	1	2	3	4	5
Stevens															
Thomas															
Valley															
Wilson															
Young															
1															
2															
3															
4															
5															
acc't.															
dent.															
law.															
phys.															
stock.															

**THE
TV NEWS PROGRAM**

by Evelyn B. Rosenthal

Butler and eight other reporters are on the staff of a TV news program aired daily Monday through Friday. Four appear every day, each with his own regular slot on the show. The other five are feature reporters; each covers a particular subject and appears once a week, on a different day, to discuss that subject. From the following clues, can you determine the full week's schedule for the program—exactly when each of the nine reporters is on the air and what area or subject he covers?

1. Archer, Ellis, and Ross—in this order, and immediately following one another—are on the air each Tuesday.

2. Gregg, Davis, and Jones—in this order, and immediately following one another— are on each Thursday.

3. Every day, sports comes after the local news and before the world news; weather comes immediately after the daily feature.

4. Clark reports on his specialty earlier in the week than Harris reports on his special feature and later in the week than the feature on health.

5. Gardening is featured earlier in the week than child psychology and later than Ross's special topic.

6. Consumerism and food, in that order, are featured on consecutive days.

You can write in the reporters' names and subjects, in the order presented (1st to 5th), in the fill-in chart below.

The solution is on page 147

	Monday	Tuesday	Wednesday	Thursday	Friday
1st					
2nd					
3rd					
4th					
5th					

27   A QUINTUPLE WEDDING

by Kathleen A. Misze

On the same date, the Brown sisters of Detroit—Betty, Cathy, Janice, Martha, and Patti—married (not necessarily respectively) Brad, Ed, Frank, George, and Steve. Each of the grooms hailed, as it happened, from a different city: Boston, Dallas, Miami, New York, or San Francisco (again in no particular order). From the following information, can you deduce the age of each bride (they were two years apart, ranging from 18 to 26), the first and last name of her bridegroom, the city he's from, and the site of each couple's honeymoon (the Grand Canyon, Hawaii, Jamaica, Paris, or Rome)?

1. Five men—Frank, Mr. Alberts, the Jamaica-bound groom, the man from Boston, and Patti's husband—all became in-laws to one another via the quintuple wedding.

2. The Grand Canyon–bound bride was the youngest, while Ed married the eldest.

3. The youngest sister's groom was not from Dallas.

4. Since it's traditional at a double (or larger) wedding that the elder or eldest woman is married first and the younger or youngest last, the order of vows were: Janice and her bridegroom, the Rome honeymooners, the man from San Francisco and his bride, the Hawaiian honeymooners, and finally George and his bride.

5. Each of the five brides carried a different kind of bouquet: Martha carried daisies; Frank's bride, roses; the Rome-bound bride, violets; Mr. Black's bride, carnations; and the bride of the man from San Francisco, mums.

6. Each of the five grooms wore a boutonniere to match his bride's bouquet: Betty's groom (Mr. Mack) wore a rose, Mr. Wilder a daisy, the man from Dallas a carnation, Mr. Jenson a mum, and Brad a violet.

7. Brad is not from Miami.

Because of its size, the solving chart had to be split into two smaller ones. It is used in the normal way, however.

The solution is on page 148.

	Brad	Ed	Frank	George	Steve	Betty	Cathy	Janice	Martha	Patti	18	20	22	24	26
Alberts															
Black															
Jenson															
Mack															
Wilder															
18															
20															
22															
24															
26															
Betty															
Cathy															
Janice															
Martha															
Patti															

	Boston	Dallas	Miami	New York	San Fran.	Grand Canyon	Hawaii	Jamaica	Paris	Rome
Brad										
Ed										
Frank										
George										
Steve										
Betty										
Cathy										
Janice										
Martha										
Patti										
Alberts										
Black										
Jenson										
Mack										
Wilder										
18										
20										
22										
24										
26										
Grand Canyon										
Hawaii										
Jamaica										
Paris										
Rome										

28 COSMETICS COSTS

by Diane Yoko

At a recent close-out sale at a local cosmetics store, Ms. Abbott, Ms. Jones, and three other women each bought one bottle of perfume (one was Divine Fragrance) and one lipstick (one was Coral Kiss). From the following clues, can you deduce each woman's full name and purchases and figure out how much each spent?

1. Helen bought Terrific Odor perfume; she spent twice as much as Ms. Smith and $4 more than Ms. Brown.

2. The woman who bought Great Smell perfume spent less than the woman who bought Tangerine Talks lipstick but more than the woman who bought Ideal Essence perfume.

3. Neither Jackie nor Ms. Brown was the one who bought Melon Mellow lipstick.

4. Sue spent twice as much as Ms. Hall, whose total was one-third of Jackie's.

5. Neither Sue nor Jackie was the woman who bought both Perfect Scent perfume and Red Moon lipstick.

6. None of the five women has the same first and last initials.

7. Ms. Smith, who is neither Jackie nor Betty, bought Pink Icing lipstick.

8. The woman who bought Melon Mellow lipstick spent $10 more than Ann.

The solution is on page 148.

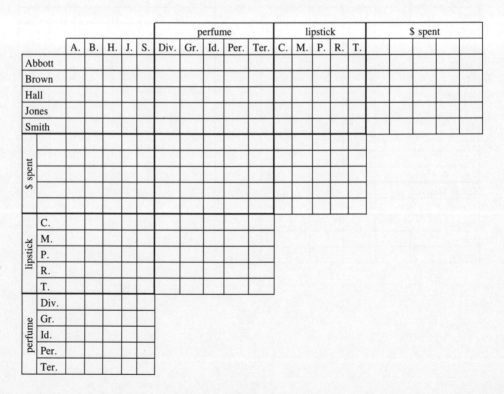

29 MOTHER–DAUGHTER BANQUET

by Faye Taylor

Five women (Mrs. Jones, Mrs. Koon, Mrs. Lee, Mrs. Mix, and Mrs. Nye) recently took their daughters (not necessarily respectively, Mrs. Able, Mrs. Best, Mrs. Cox, Mrs. Dill, and Mrs. Eton) to the annual Retired Women's Club Mother-Daughter Banquet. As it happens, each of the mothers sat at a different table (each mother sat with her own daughter); the tables were numbered 1 through 5. Among the daughters, all accomplished young women, are an accountant, an attorney, an engineer, a pharmacist, and a professor. From the following clues, can you match each club member with her daughter, give each daughter's occupation, and determine the table at which each mother-daughter pair sat?

1. The attorney's mother and Mrs. Lee and Mrs. Cox's mother all have grandchildren; the mother at table 1 and Mrs. Nye do not.

2. Mrs. Dill is expecting her first child in the next few months; the professor does not plan to have children for several years.

3. The engineer, who is not Mrs. Cox, did not sit at table 3.

4. Mrs. Nye and her daughter, who is not the professor, did not sit at table 2 or table 5.

5. Mrs. Mix, whose daughter is not an attorney or a pharmacist, and Mrs. Jones could talk about their grandchildren for hours.

6. Mrs. Able and Mrs. Eton have children at the same school.

7. Mrs. Eton and the attorney and the daughter at table 5 all attended the same college.

8. The grandmother at table 3 was not Mrs. Jones.

The solution is on page 149.

	Able	Best	Cox	Dill	Eton	1	2	3	4	5	acc't.	attor.	eng.	phar.	prof.
Jones															
Koon															
Lee															
Mix															
Nye															
acc't.															
attor.															
eng.															
phar.															
prof.															
1															
2															
3															
4															
5															

30 CONDO COMPLEX

by Dodi Schultz

The Quades and five other married couples occupy the six apartments at the one-story condominium called the Clover Arms. One husband's first name is George. The complex includes a swimming pool and a tennis court and, as shown in the accompanying diagram, each apartment has two entrances—one from a path leading from the street, the other giving directly upon either the tennis court or the pool. From the following clues, can you find the full names of the couple in each of the numbered units?

1. Ira's apartment is on the tennis-court side.

2. Agatha's apartment immediately adjoins those of the Parkers and the Riders.

3. Bruce and his wife, who are not the Newells, live north of at least one other couple.

4. Edward and Frances live in different wings.

5. Laura, whose apartment is not on the pool side, lives south of the Newells.

6. Mrs. Minton and her husband, who is not Jeffrey, are closer to the tennis court than Harriet, who is not Mrs. O'Brian.

7. Carol lives to the east of at least one other couple.

8. Kate, who is not Mrs. Rider, has farther to walk to the pool than Bruce.

9. The Riders live north of at least one other couple.

10. Donald, whose wife is not Frances, lives west of the O'Brians.

11. Edward's apartment is closer to the pool than at least one other.

12. At least one couple lives south of the Parkers.

The solution is on page 149.

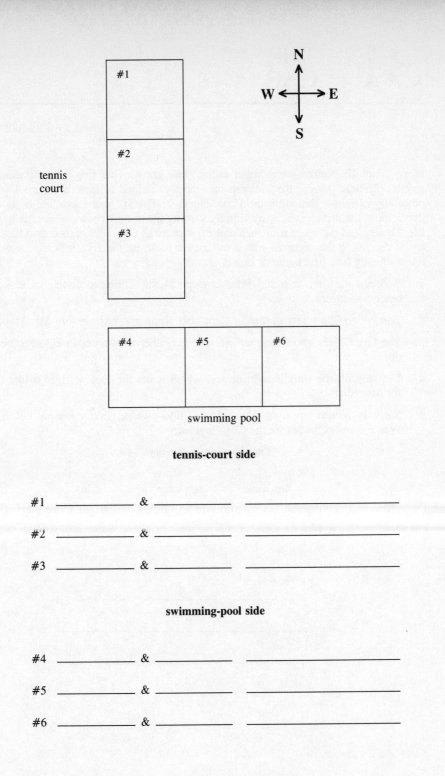

tennis court

#1

#2

#3

swimming pool

#4   #5   #6

tennis-court side

#1 _____ & _____   _____

#2 _____ & _____   _____

#3 _____ & _____   _____

swimming-pool side

#4 _____ & _____   _____

#5 _____ & _____   _____

#6 _____ & _____   _____

31 THE CAR POOL

by Lois Bohnsack

Since Granville, unlike some larger cities, does not provide free transportation for its elected officials, Mayor Roy Thompson recently decided to form a car pool with five other city officials, including the Parks Director. The six share gasoline costs and the mayor does the driving since, by slightly varying his normal route, he is able to pick up Mr. Dewey and the other four men and drive them to City Hall. From the clues below, try to determine the order in which the mayor picks up the five officials, and the full name of each (the first name of one is David).

1. Between the first stop and Frank's stop, Mayor Thompson acquires at least two other passengers.

2. The Police Chief gets in the car right after Keith and right before Mr. Trent.

3. The Fire Chief, who is not Mr. Morris, is neither the first nor the last to be picked up.

4. The stop for the Buildings Inspector, which is not the first, is right before the stop for Mr. Eller.

5. Steve is picked up right after Mr. Ashton—whose first name is not Keith or Walter—and right before the City Engineer.

The solution is on page 149.

	first name	last name	title
1st	_____	_____	_____
2nd	_____	_____	_____
3rd	_____	_____	_____
4th	_____	_____	_____
5th	_____	_____	_____

32 PLAYING THE STOCK MARKET

by Randall L. Whipkey

One recent morning, Lucky Louie decided to try the stock market as a means of increasing his fortune, so he bought shares in five corporations, scientifically choosing his stocks by throwing darts at a newspaper listing. As Lucky Louie would have it, all five stocks rose in price by the end of that day. From the following clues, can you deduce how much each stock increased in value and its closing price at the end of the day? (No two increases or closing prices were the same.)

1. Polk Motors stock increased 2 points more than Zeroz Corp. stock, while its closing price was 10 points less than the Zeroz stock and one-half that of the highest-priced stock.

2. Nadir Markets increased twice as much as Siding Aluminum to a closing price four times that of Siding stock.

3. The stock with the third-highest closing price went up twice as many points as Black Gold Petroleum stock, which closed 5 points higher than the lowest-priced stock; the smallest increase was 2 points.

4. The lowest-priced stock closed 25 points under the third-highest-priced one.

5. The highest-priced stock increased 1 point less than the Black Gold Petroleum stock.

The solution is on page 150.

	increases					closing prices				
Black Gold										
Nadir										
Polk										
Siding										
Zeroz										
closing prices										

33 FRIENDS AND ACTIVITIES

by Karen Feinberg

In River City there live five women friends who, among them, like to do five things in their spare time. Each one likes two of the five activities and shares each of her interests with one of her friends. From the clues given below, can you figure out each woman's full name (one first name is Gail) and the two forms of recreation she likes best?

1. Holly and Ms. Orr go cycling together.

2. Ellie goes to baseball games with Ms. Munn, who is Fran's neighbor.

3. Neither Ms. Nye nor Ms. King plays golf.

4. Ms. Lane shares one interest with Ellie and another with Jane.

5. Ms. Munn, who is not Jane, has no interest in cycling.

6. Ms. King goes canoeing with one of the baseball fans.

7. One of the moviegoers is a baseball fan and the other plays golf with Jane.

We used both charts to solve this puzzle, one to keep track of the first names and last names, and the fill-in chart to write in which two women enjoyed each activity.

The solution is on page 150.

	Ellie	Fran	Gail	Holly	Jane
King					
Lane					
Munn					
Nye					
Orr					

baseball _____ & _____

canoeing _____ & _____

cycling   _____ & _____

golf   _____ & _____

movies   _____ & _____

34   A RACE TO THE FINISH

by Cheryl McLaughlin

The first race at Hilltop Track featured ten riders, including Cathy Cash and Adam. From the clues, can you determine each rider's full name, the horse each rode (one is named Foxy Lady), and their places in the race?

1. Finishing first through fifth, respectively, were Johnson riding Lucky, Smith, Karen, Doyle, and Kane.

2. Brown's horse (which was not Katie Bell) finished in last place, just a nose behind Hopeful.

3. Hanson finished five places ahead of Sue.

4. Jubilee came in two places behind Henry's horse, but two places ahead of the horse ridden by Mr. Bates.

5. Pete and John rode Katie Bell and Penny Money, not necessarily respectively; Pete finished the race ahead of John.

6. Delaware; Ed's horse, Kitty Kat; and Potts's horse finished consecutively, in that order.

7. Jack's horse finished *directly* ahead of Best Boy, who finished two places ahead of the horse ridden by Chuck.

8. Mr. Farrell's horse finished ahead of Prideful.

The solution is on page 151.

HILLTOP TRACK RESULTS

	rider's name		horse's name
	first	last	
1st			
2nd			
3rd			
4th			
5th			
6th			
7th			
8th			
9th			
10th			

HARD LOGIC PROBLEMS

35 CONSUMER COUPONS

by Edna M. McNellis

Last year, five companies distributed coupons offering either a cash rebate or a free product to consumers who mailed them in with proof of purchase. The five coupons each had a different expiration date—January 31, March 15, May 1, October 31, or December 31 of last year. From the following clues, can you find the product each company produces (one is soap), the amount of each cash rebate (one was 75¢), and the expiration date for each offer?

1. Strong did not offer the $2 rebate, and the firm's coupon was neither the first nor the last to expire.

2. The cosmetics coupon expired before Abbot's offer, but after the $1 rebate.

3. Neither the $2 rebate nor Clark's offer expired on the last day of any month.

4. The cereal rebate expired on October 31.

5. The following expired in consecutive order: B&D's coupon, the offer on bread, and the $1.50 rebate offer.

6. Clark's offer was not on cosmetics, and Folk's was not on paper towels.

7. Abbot offered a free product.

The solution is on page 151.

	bread	cereal	cosmetics	paper	soap	value					1/31	3/15	5/1	10/31	12/31
Abbot															
B&D															
Clark															
Folk															
Strong															
1/31															
3/15															
5/1															
10/31															
12/31															
value															

73

36 THE VOYAGES

by Haydon Calhoun

In 1392, the tiny Pacific queendom of Howareya was flat broke and had no natural resources, so Queen Lulu hocked her jewels for 42,000 simoleons to build four ships which sailed in all four directions in search of wealth. Naturally, she had hoped they would find gold, spices, tobacco, or even "that messy, smelly, oily stuff," but instead, her ship captains, the zany Marco brothers, discovered only the Banana, the Coconut, the Orange, and the Pineapple islands—ingredients for a fruit salad, but not the riches she had sought. Little did she know at the time that those fruits would soon make her tiny queendom the "Fruit Salad Capital of the World" and rich beyond her wildest dreams. From the clues below, match each Marco brother with the name of his ship, its cost (no two cost the same), the direction he sailed, the island he discovered, and the duration (each was different) of each voyage.

1. The cheapest ship made the shortest voyage, 15 days; the longest voyage was 40 days, in a ship that cost 2000 simoleons more.

2. Zippo's voyage was twice as long as the northern voyage, which was not the shortest voyage or the voyage of the ship *Duck Soup*.

3. Harko did not make the shortest voyage, which was not to the east.

4. Gaucho's ship cost 12,000 simoleons.

5. The southern voyage was twice as long as the voyage made by the 6000-simoleon ship *Animal Crackers*.

6. Chito was not the captain of the *Monkey Business*.

7. Chito's ship cost 6000 simoleons less than the *Duck Soup*, which cost less than the *Horse Feathers*.

8. The voyage to Coconut Island was half as long as the voyage to Pineapple Island.

9. The ship that discovered Orange Island cost more than the ship that made the longest voyage, to Banana Island.

The chart, which had to be divided because of its size, is used in the regular way.

The solution is on page 151.

	Animal	Duck	Horse	Monkey	cost				N	S	E	W
Chito												
Gaucho												
Harko												
Zippo												
days 15												
40												
Banana												
Coconut												
Orange												
Pine.												
N												
S												
E												
W												
cost												

	Banana	Coconut	Orange	Pine.	days 15			40
Chito								
Gaucho								
Harko								
Zippo								

37 MINIATURE GOLF

by Jennifer Stern

Carl and three friends played a four-hole course of miniature golf. Each one chose a different color ball; one was green. The par scores for the four holes, in order, were 2, 3, 3, and 2. From the following clues, can you determine the ball each player used, the score he made on each hole, and the final winning order? (*Note:* In golf, high score loses, since the object is to use as few strokes as possible; "par" is the course's established decent score for each hole and for the course as a whole.)

1. The player of the blue ball made the only two holes-in-one (balls sunk with only one stroke), on the first and fourth holes.

2. Bob's total was under seven.

3. The player of the red ball, who was not Dan, went over par on two holes but totaled precisely par at the end.

4. One player scored two on each of the first three holes.

5. The only time Dan, who took third place and did not play the yellow ball, went over par was when he shot four on the second hole.

6. Alan shot six on the last hole.

The solution is on page 152.

		blue	green	red	yellow	1st	2nd	3rd	4th	1	2	3	4	TOTAL
										\multicolumn{5}{c}{score / hole}
Alan														
Bob														
Carl														
Dan														
score	hole 1													
	hole 2													
	hole 3													
	hole 4													
	TOTAL													
1st														
2nd														
3rd														
4th														

38 ANNIVERSARY PARTY

by Diane C. Baldwin

The four siblings of the Green family—two brothers and two sisters—and their spouses got together to celebrate the anniversary of one of the couples. The three couples who were not having anniversaries each brought a different gift for the honored couple (one gift was theater tickets). From the following clues can you find the full names of all four couples (one husband is Bill, and two surnames are Smith and Stout), identify the anniversary couple, and determine what gift each of the other couples brought?

Note: In this problem you may assume (a) that the wives all adopted their husbands' last names, and (b) that a spouse's sibling's spouse may be termed an in-law.

1. Jean and her husband brought a gift, but it wasn't champagne.

2. Joan's sister is married to Harry's wife's brother, who is not George.

3. Harry's surname is not Stout, and his wife is not Jean.

4. Two couples who brought gifts were Nancy and her husband, and Paul and his wife; their gifts, not necessarily respectively, were a bottle of champagne and a basket of fruit.

5. Jean's only brother-in-law and his wife, Jane, were not celebrating their anniversary.

The solution is on page 152.

husband's first	wife's first	last name	gift brought

39 THE HOME-RUN CHAMPS

by Fred H. Dale

Five players in the Northwest Baseball Association had phenomenal slugging records last season. They all hit 32 or more home runs, and their batting averages ranged from 300 to 316 (no two men had the same home-run record or batting average). The home-run champion set a new Association record of 40. As it happens, all the statistics are even numbers and, without exception, the men who hit more home runs had lower batting averages—that is, the men's ranking by batting averages is in reverse order to their ranking by homers. With the aid of the following clues, you should be able to determine the batting average and the number of home runs hit by each.

1. Warner's batting average was 10 points higher than Banks's.

2. Rodgers was halfway between Jensen and Banks in home runs, but he was halfway between Jensen and South in batting average.

3. Banks was halfway between Jensen and Warner in home runs, but he was halfway between Rodgers and South in batting average.

The solution is on page 153.

The solution is on page 153.

	home runs				batting average				
	32			40	300				316
Banks									
Jensen									
Rodgers									
South									
Warner									
300					
316					

(average)

78

40 NEWSPAPER FEATURES

by Evelyn B. Rosenthal

Each of New City's three daily papers, which publish Monday through Saturday, has two special departments that it features on certain days. No two papers run any of the same special features. Each paper carries one or both of its features on three days and has only the usual news coverage on the other three. From the following clues, can you find the topics featured by each paper (one is *The Bugle*) and the days on which each topic appears?

1. On Tuesday, only *The Eagle,* which features food news, has more than the usual news coverage.

2. Business is featured three times a week, travel only on Wednesday, and each of the other topics twice a week.

3. A different pair of topics is featured each day; theater and music news appear in different papers on Saturday.

4. *The Clarion* has more than the usual news coverage on Monday, Thursday, and Saturday; on Thursday it is the only paper that does.

5. Society and theater news are not featured by the same paper.

The solution is on page 153.

	Mon.	Tues.	Wed.	Thurs.	Fri.	Sat.
Bugle						
Clarion						
Eagle						

41 CIRCUS TIME

by Kathleen A. Misze

Dan, Fred, Harry, John, and Marty, who are (not necessarily respectively) a bareback rider, a clown, an elephant trainer, a lion tamer, and a trapeze artist, perform the five acts that (in one order or another) form the finale of each afternoon's performance at the Bingling Brothers Circus; they are known professionally as "Dancy Dart," "Flash," "Juda Jewel," "Pompy," and "Skip"—again, not necessarily respectively. In his act, each of the five men has a partner, who happens to be the wife of one of the other four. (Each of the five wives has taken her husband's last name.) From the following information, can you determine each performer's last name (variously, Beach, Heron, Hogan, Miller, or Smith), his professional name, his act, and his partner's full name, as well as the order in which the five acts are presented?

1. Christine isn't "Flash's" partner.

2. The five married couples are "Skip" and Christine Miller, Marty and Marsha Beach, Harry and Claudia, Mr. Hogan and the trapeze artist's partner, and Fred and Nancy.

3. Harry isn't "Dancy Dart."

4. The women's order of appearance in the show is as follows: Sharon, Mrs. Smith, "Juda Jewel's" partner, John's partner, and Claudia.

5. The men appear in the following order: Claudia's husband, Marty, Mr. Smith, "Flash," and the lion tamer.

6. Nancy isn't married to the elephant trainer.

7. "Flash" is the most experienced circus performer, while the elephant trainer has the least experience, and the clown falls in between.

The solution is on page 154.

	performer	prof. name	act	partner
1st				
2nd				
3rd				
4th				
5th				

42 FLYING FROM NEW YORK TO FLORIDA

by Evelyn B. Rosenthal

One recent morning, a number of flights left from the three airports that serve New York City to fly to either Miami or Fort Lauderdale, Florida. Carlson and five other pilots flew different routes; that is, no two of them left and landed at the same pair of airports. From the following clues, describing the flights that morning, can you find the number of flights on each route and which route was flown by each of the six pilots?

1. The smallest number of flights, four, was on Benson's route.

2. On the run to Miami, there were as many flights from LaGuardia as from John F. Kennedy and Newark together.

3. Ewig and Fox did not fly from the same airport.

4. There was the same number of flights to each of the Florida destinations.

5. There were twice as many flights on Fox's route as on Allen's.

6. Of the Fort Lauderdale flights, there were two fewer from LaGuardia than from JFK and two more from LaGuardia than from Newark.

7. The total number of flights on Allen's and Ewig's routes was the same as the total on Benson's and Dawson's.

8. The total number of flights from Newark to Miami was the same as the number from LaGuardia to Fort Lauderdale.

Use the space below for solving.

The solution is on page 154

43 SEMINARY GRADUATES

by Gary Maeder

Each of the top five students in the recent graduating class of a leading theological seminary on the West Coast is pursuing a different vocation. One of them is continuing his education at the seminary in order to get a doctorate and then teach in a seminary somewhere in the U.S. The others, in no particular order, have become a church pastor, a university chaplain, a marriage counselor, and an overseas missionary. The first names of the five, in alphabetical order, are Eric, Jeff, Pete, Roy, and Ted. Their last names, again in alphabetical order, are Anderson, Brentley, Carter, Evans, and Jacobsen. Given this information and the clues below, can you determine each graduate's complete name, current vocation, and rank in his class?

1. The future seminary professor and the fifth-ranking student grew up in the same city and attended the same church as children.

2. Since Jacobsen, whose first name is not Jeff, and Pete were single, they roomed together throughout their three years in the seminary.

3. Ted considered becoming a university chaplain but decided against it.

4. Carter ranked three places higher than Ted, while Pete bested the future seminary professor by two notches. The remaining student in the top five, who is now the church pastor, has become well known for a book he wrote while still in seminary.

5. The dean of the seminary performed the weddings of Roy, Evans, and the student who is now the university chaplain while they were in their second year of seminary. None of the three has any plans for further study at the seminary.

6. Neither Brentley nor Evans intends to leave the U.S. in the foreseeable future.

The solution is on page 154.

	Eric	Jeff	Pete	Roy	Ted	1st	2nd	3rd	4th	5th	prof.	pastor	chaplain	marr. c.	mission.
Anderson															
Brentley															
Carter															
Evans															
Jacobsen															
prof.										
pastor										
chaplain										
marr. c.										
mission.										
1st					
2nd					
3rd					
4th					
5th					

44 PRACTICE MAKES PERFECT

by Cheryl McLaughlin

Barb and five of her friends have recently been taking lessons in different activities. From the following clues, can you determine each girl's full name (one surname is Smith), her activity, and the number of months she has been taking lessons? (*Note: No fractions of months are involved.*)

1. Jenny and the Sweet girl practice their dance and piano lessons together.

2. Ginger has taken lessons one month longer than the Jensen girl (who is not Laurie).

3. Cathy Brown has taken lessons six months longer than the dancer and ten months longer than the Baker girl, who golfs.

4. The tennis player has taken lessons for five months—longer than Sue and the skater, but not as long as Ginger, or the swimmer, or the girl who has taken lessons for twenty months.

5. The dancer has taken lessons twice as long as the Johnson girl and three times as long as Sue.

The solution is on page 155.

	B.	C.	G.	J.	L.	S.	months						dance	golf	piano	skate	swim	tennis
Baker																		
Brown																		
Jensen																		
Johnson																		
Smith																		
Sweet																		
dance																		
golf																		
piano																		
skate																		
swim																		
tennis																		

months

45 THE FAMILY PETS

by Evelyn B. Rosenthal

The Days collectively own five pets of different kinds; each family member assumes responsibility for feeding and caring for one of the five animals. From the following clues, can you find the first name of each of the Days (one is Val), the kind of animal he or she cares for (one is a bird), and the pet's name (one is Gog)?

1. Mr. and Mrs. Day are the same age.

2. The one who cares for the dog is the same age as Chris and the same sex as Pat and the one who cares for Tip.

3. The older son, who is not one of the twins, takes care of the hamster.

4. Neither of the parents cares for the rabbit.

5. The one who takes care of the cat is the same age as Sal and the same sex as the one who cares for Dibs.

6. Lee, who is not one of the twins, takes care of Flip.

7. No one is the same age as the one who takes care of Jiggs.

8. Dibs is not the rabbit.

9. Not all the children are boys.

We did not find a chart to be helpful in solving this puzzle. Use the space below to write down facts as you determine them.

The solution is on page 155.

46 THE MARTIAL ARTS

by Haydon Calhoun

Due to the growing interest in Oriental self-defense techniques, the Central City YMCA has added three classes—judo, karate, and kung fu—to its athletic program. Along with the regular classes—boxing and wrestling—each class is held one evening a week, Monday through Friday. The five instructors, who have nonathletic daytime jobs, are named (in no special order) Hale, Hardy, Power, Stout, and Strong. Their first names (again, not respectively) are Albert, Clarence, Edwin, Homer, and Waldo. From the following clues, try to determine the order in which the five classes are held, the first and last name of each instructor, and his daytime job.

1. The accountant and the wrestler do not hold their classes on consecutive days.

2. The printer instructs his class later in the week than either Stout or the druggist, but before the kung fu instructor.

3. Strong, who teaches earlier in the week than the jeweler, holds his class two days after the librarian.

4. The five men conduct classes as follows: Waldo, the day after Hale and two days before Power; Edwin, two days after the boxer.

5. Strong, who coaches later in the week than Homer, has an interest in Albert's area of expertise as well as his own, and often drops in to watch the latter's classes.

6. Last week in their respective classes, Waldo and the karate instructor brought in some professionals for a few exhibition matches.

The solution is on page 156.

The solution is on page 156.

	instructor		occupation	class taught
Mon.	_____	_____	_____	_____
Tues.	_____	_____	_____	_____
Wed.	_____	_____	_____	_____
Thur.	_____	_____	_____	_____
Fri.	_____	_____	_____	_____

47 ONCE-A-WEEK TREAT

by Diane Yoko

Every Friday morning, Helen and four of her colleagues stop at bakeries and buy treats to have during their coffee break. One woman is a customer of Dandy Dough Bakery. From the following clues about last week's purchases, can you determine the full name of each woman (one surname is Adams), the bakery she goes to, the kind of treat she bought, and the price she paid?

1. Paula's Danish was not bought at Yummy Yum Bakery.

2. Ms. Forest has never been to Baker's Best Bakery.

3. The treat bought at Goody Good Bakery and the Danish were the same price, which was cheaper than at least one other treat.

4. The cinnamon twist cost twice as much as the treat bought at Yummy Yum Bakery but 10¢ less than the crescent roll.

5. Ms. Wilson's treat cost less than Dot's.

6. The doughnut bought at Tasty Treat Bakery cost 5¢ more than the cherry-filled bismarck, which was 20¢ less than Ms. Hacket's treat, which wasn't the most expensive.

7. Paula's last name isn't Hacket.

8. Ms. Hart's treat cost more than the one bought at Baker's Best Bakery.

9. Jane's treat cost more than the doughnut but less than the one Sandy bought.

The chart, divided because of its size, is used in the regular way.

The solution is on page 156.

	Dot	Helen	Jane	Paula	Sandy	price					bism.	cin. tw.	cres.	Dan.	dough
Adams															
Forest															
Hacket															
Hart															
Wilson															
BB															
DD															
GG															
TT															
YY															
bism.															
cin. tw.															
cres.															
Dan.															
dough.															
price															

	BB	DD	GG	TT	YY
Adams					
Forest					
Hacket					
Hart					
Wilson					

48 THE BASKETBALL LEAGUE

by Randall L. Whipkey

In this year's Summerset Elementary School Basketball League, each of the six teams entered played each of the others one time, and each compiled a different record (number of wins and losses) for the season. From the clues below, can you deduce the order in which the teams placed, each team's nickname (one is the Orioles), and its coach (one is Nichols)?

1. West Elementary lost only to the Robins, who are not coached by Lewis.

2. The Cardinals beat both South Elementary and the team coached by Kilmer but lost to the Falcons.

3. Suburban Elementary lost to the Hawks but defeated Osgood's team.

4. Central Elementary defeated Miller's squad.

5. Kilmer doesn't coach the Hawks.

6. North defeated James's team, which isn't the Cardinals.

7. West's nickname isn't the Hawks.

8. Neither Osgood nor James coaches South.

9. East's nickname isn't the Eagles.

The solution is on page 157.

The solution is on page 157.

	Card.	Eag.	Fal.	Hawks	Orio.	Rob.	James	Kilmer	Lewis	Miller	Nich.	Osg.	1st	2nd	3rd	4th	5th	6th
Central																		
East																		
North																		
South																		
Suburb.																		
West																		
1st													
2nd													
3rd													
4th													
5th													
6th													
James							
Kilmer							
Lewis							
Miller							
Nich.							
Osg.							

49 JOHN'S GUESSES

by Evelyn B. Rosenthal

When John was a member of the panel from which trial jurors were being selected, he diverted himself while waiting by trying to guess the sort of job held by Edward and five other jurors who were being questioned about their qualifications, and then checking his guesses against the answers they gave. From the following clues, can you find the full names of the six (one surname is Faber), the category of work each does, and John's guess about each?

1. John guessed correctly the numbers of white-collar workers, blue-collar workers, and professionals, which were all different, but he was right about only two individuals, Chris and Ms. Butler.

2. Sue and Ryder are the only blue-collar workers among the six.

3. John assigned each of the white-collar workers to a different work classification from any other white-collar worker.

4. He was wrong in his identification of both Pat and Olsen, who are, in fact, white-collar workers.

5. Lee, whose surname is not Tonks, is a professional.

6. John guessed that Dale was a blue-collar worker and that King was a professional.

Note the blank boxes given with "actual" and "guess" rows and columns. While solving, we entered either a W (white), B (blue) or P (professional) into the box as it was established. We found this helpful.

The solution is on page 157.

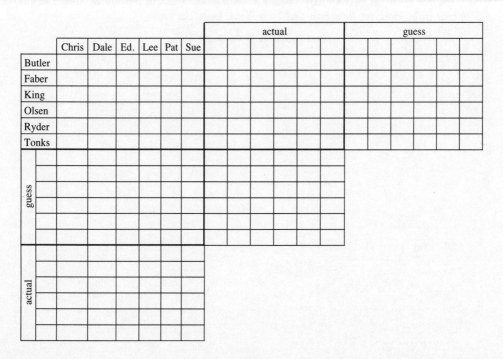

50 THE TRAVEL AGENTS

by Haydon Calhoun

Seven friends and alumni of the University of Geneva—Dino, Hans, Kirk, Toby, Van, Willy, and Yancy—are international travel and tourism agents. One lives and works in New York City, while the others are each headquartered in a different European city. During a particular calendar year, the New Yorker spent six consecutive months on business in Europe, where he visited a different one of his six friends each month. Likewise, each of his six friends made a trip to New York to visit him during a different month in that same calendar year. From the clues below, try to determine each agent's home city, the month in which each European visited the New Yorker, and the month the New Yorker visited each of his European friends.

1. Kirk visited the New Yorker in March, whereas the five other friends visited him as follows: the Londoner, the month after the friend from Madrid; Willy, the month before the Parisian and seven months after Toby.

2. Three of the men—Van, Hans, and the Londoner—visited the New Yorker for two weeks.

3. The friend who was in New York the month after Kirk could visit only during the last week of that month, so the New Yorker went home with him to Stockholm for the first month of his European tour.

4. The Berliner and the friend who visited the New Yorker in November had both been in New York before; it was the first visit for both Van and the friend who visited the month after Willy.

5. The New Yorker visited Dino five months after he saw him in New York.

6. The New Yorker had already visited Rome before he spent the fourth month of his tour in Madrid; he flew home to New York from Berlin.

The solution is on page 157.

Jan. _____ _____

Feb. _____ _____

Mar. _____ _____

Apr. _____ _____

May _____ _____

June _____ _____

July _____ _____

Aug. _____ _____

Sept. _____ _____

Oct. _____ _____

Nov. _____ _____

Dec. _____ _____

	Dino	Hans	Kirk	Toby	Van	Willy	Yancy
Berlin							
London							
Madrid							
New York							
Paris							
Rome							
Stock.							

51 WEDDING ANNIVERSARIES

by Virginia C. McCarthy

Constance and four other married women were recently discussing wedding anniversaries and, in so doing, discovered that their own anniversaries occur in five consecutive months. From the following clues, can you find the full names of all five (one last name is Newman) and their anniversaries (both months and dates)? *Note:* April, June, September, and November have 30 days; February has 28 or 29 days; and the other months have 31 days. A perfect square is the result of a number multiplied by itself, i.e., 2 × 2 = 4 (a perfect square).

1. One of the anniversaries is in May; none is in August.

2. Both Faith's and Mrs. Williams's anniversary dates are even multiples of five, but only Faith's is also a multiple of three.

3. Prudence's anniversary, which is not in July, is exactly 36 days after Mrs. Lawton's.

4. Hope's anniversary comes earliest in the year and before the 20th of the month.

5. Two anniversaries are less than ten days apart, and a third anniversary is on the 31st of the month.

6. Mrs. Dowling's anniversary date is an odd number divisible by seven.

7. Verity's anniversary date is a two-digit perfect square.

8. Mrs. Swanson's first name is not Faith.

The solution is on page 158.

	Constance	Faith	Hope	Prudence	Verity	month					day				
Dowling															
Lawton															
Newman															
Swanson															
Williams															

(day)

(month)

52

THREE BY THREE

by Dodi Schultz

As youngsters, the Feltons and the other two sets of triplets in Tinyville, all close in age, naturally became friends, and they had something in common beyond their special family status: all were ardent flying enthusiasts. In fact, when they grew up, Arthur and the other eight did take to the skies; each holds one of the three airline positions mentioned in the clues below. Can you find the full names and jobs of all nine?

1. George is a pilot, as is Frank's sister.
2. Ida's sister is a flight attendant, as is Helen's brother.
3. David is a copilot, as is Ethel's sister.
4. Only one of Carol's brothers is a pilot.
5. Betty's brother is a copilot; her sister is not.
6. None of the Melton triplets is a copilot.
7. One and only one in each family is a flight attendant.
8. In one family, two siblings of the same sex have the same job; they are not the Peltons.

The solution is on page 159.

The solution is on page 159.

Felton		Melton		Pelton	

53

THE NEW APARTMENTS

by Nancy R. Patterson

Mike, Olivia, and four other employees transferred by Amalgamated Airways felt fortunate to locate apartments in the same new building near the airport. The three-story building has two apartments to a floor: 1A and 1B are on the first floor, 2A and 2B on the second, and 3A and 3B on the third. Apartments lettered A face the street, while those lettered B face the garden at the back of the building. From the clues below, can you deduce each employee's full name (one last name is Endicott) and his or her apartment number?

1. Lisa's apartment faces the same way as Corwin's, but Corwin isn't directly above her.

2. Dutton's apartment faces the garden.

3. Kay shares her floor, which isn't the third, with Forney.

4. The persons in 2A and 3B are of opposite sexes.

5. Neil's apartment is one floor above Gorman's and faces in the opposite direction.

6. Two women's apartments face the street.

7. Peter's and Forney's apartments face the same way.

8. Lisa isn't Hill.

9. Kay isn't Gorman.

10. None of the men has an apartment directly over another man's.

The solution is on page 159.

	Kay	Lisa	Olivia	Mike	Neil	Peter
Corwin						
Dutton						
Endicott						
Forney						
Gorman						
Hill						

3A	3B
2A	2B

street   1A   1B   garden

54 THE TALENT SHOW

by Cheryl McLaughlin

The Glenside Community School recently held a talent show, with one participant from each of the grades one through ten; each child had been previously selected as an outstanding performer in his or her class. As it happens, Cindy and Mike and the other eight youngsters represented just five families, each of which has exactly two children. One family's name is Keyes. From the following clues, can you pinpoint the performer representing each grade, and give the full name of all five families? One mother is Linda, and one father is Vic. (*Note: You may assume that all the children are in the usual grades—e.g., that children three grades apart are three years apart in age.*)

1. The children from youngest to oldest are: one of Randy's children; Kathy Irons; one of Steve and Monica's daughters; the Jones boys; one of the Gaines children; Pam's daughter; Sally, who has a sister; Pam's son; and Ted's son.

2. Nancy, who is not Mrs. Gaines, took her son and daughter out for ice cream after the show.

3. A girl named Hughes is seven years older than Alice.

4. Olive is not Mrs. Gaines.

5. Bob is one year younger than Jimmy, while there is a four-year difference between Jimmy and Chuck; four years also separate Bob and Alice.

6. Wayne's daughter is Cheryl.

7. John has a sister.

The solution is on page 159.

	father's first	mother's first	family's last	child's first
10				
9				
8				
7				
6				
5				
4				
3				
2				
1				

father's first	mother's first	family's last	children	grade

55 NEW CAREERS

by Nancy R. Patterson

Thanks to a workshop for returning-to-work homemakers sponsored by the Riverton Women's Resource Center, Ginny and four other women have launched new careers. Each participant in the workshop discovered that her previous experience, no matter how slight, qualified her for some job or some educational opportunity that appealed to her. From the following clues, can you determine each woman's full name and street, her previous experience, and her new field?

1. Jody and Ms. Field, who both have young children, share an apartment on Oak Street.

2. The woman who lives on Elm Street is a widow.

3. One of the five now sells real estate; she is not Ms. King.

4. Marge, who is not Ms. Holt or Ms. Smith, had dropped out of nursing school when she married. Although still happily married, she joined the workshop seeking a new challenge now that her children are grown.

5. The divorced woman who lives on Tenth Street, who is not Ms. Wilks, now works in a day-care center.

6. A widow whose only experience was managing the family finances now works as a bank teller.

7. Ruth, whose two children are both in college, does not live on Tenth Street.

8. Two of the workshop participants have become full-time students: one is taking a paralegal course and the other, who lives on Maple Street, is studying to become a medical technician.

9. Claudia, Ms. Holt, and Ms. Smith all attended the workshop longer than the woman with experience in typing, who is divorced.

10. The woman whose only experience was in club work, whose surname is neither Smith nor Field, does not live on Tenth Street.

11. Ms. King, who is not Ginny, is neither the woman with training in nursing nor the one with training in nutrition.

Use the split chart in the same way as a regular solving chart.

The solution is on page 160.

	Claudia	Ginny	Jody	Marge	Ruth	then					now				
						club	family	nurse	nutr.	typing	day c.	med.	para.	r. est.	teller
Field															
Holt															
King															
Smith															
Wilks															
now day c.															
now med.															
now para.															
now r. est.															
now teller															
then club															
then family															
then nurse															
then nutr.															
then typing															

	street				
	Elm	Maple	Oak	Oak	Tenth
Claudia					
Ginny					
Jody					
Marge					
Ruth					
Field					
Holt					
King					
Smith					
Wilks					
now day c.					
now med.					
now para.					
now r. est.					
now teller					
then club					
then family					
then nurse					
then nutr.					
then typing					

56 TOPICS FOR DISCUSSION

by Evelyn B. Rosenthal

Fran and four other children are in the same home room at school. Each day of the week, their teacher devotes the home-room period to a discussion of a different subject; each of the five children likes a different day best and a different day least. From the following clues, can you find the subject discussed each day, each child's full name (one surname is Nelson) and sex, and the days he or she likes and dislikes most?

1. Each of the boys likes a current-events day best; the discussions they like least are the three in the middle of the week.

2. The Fisher child's favorite topic, "Morality in Everyday Life," comes later in the week than "Conservation," which is not the Parker child's favorite.

3. The day Lee dislikes most comes two days after the one Chris dislikes.

4. No two of the three current-events days are consecutive; the discussion of national current events comes earlier in the week than that of foreign current events.

5. Pat and the Drew child are the only two whose best and worst ratings are not for two consecutive days.

6. Local current events is not disliked most by a girl.

7. The Abbot child's best- and least-liked days are each respectively later in the week than Val's and earlier than those of the child who likes local current events least.

8. The days Chris and Lee like most are not consecutive.

The fill-in chart below is what we used to solve this Logic Problem. The lines are for each child's first and last name, to be filled in as determined.

The solution is on page 160.

	Monday	Tuesday	Wednesday	Thursday	Friday
most liked	———— ————	———— ————	———— ————	———— ————	———— ————
least liked	———— ————	———— ————	———— ————	———— ————	———— ————
topic					

57 THE TOP FIVE HITS

by Julie Spence

For five straight weeks, the same five songs held the top five positions at radio station KJKJ, although each song was in a different position each of the five weeks. From the information below, can you determine how each song ranked each week?

1. The first week "Beverly's Song" ranked after "Evening Has Shattered," but it was not in last place.

2. "Tiptoe Through the Violets" was one place higher the third week than it had been the second week.

3. "Evening Has Shattered" was higher the second week than it was either the first or fourth week.

4. "Age of Sagittarius" was in first place two weeks later than it was in second place.

5. "Age of Sagittarius," which never ranked just one below "Tiptoe Through the Violets," fell one position from the fourth to the fifth week.

6. "Burning Chariots," which was lower than "Evening Has Shattered" in the fourth week, was one higher than this song the last week.

The solution is on page 161.

Note: In the chart the rankings read across, the weeks read down.

	"Age"					"Beverly"					"Burning"					"Evening"					"Tiptoe"				
week	1st	2nd	3rd	4th	5th	1st	2nd	3rd	4th	5th	1st	2nd	3rd	4th	5th	1st	2nd	3rd	4th	5th	1st	2nd	3rd	4th	5th
1																									
2																									
3																									
4																									
5																									

58 DEAL OF THE CARDS

by Tara Lynn Fulton

A card dealer has shuffled the jacks, queens, kings, and aces from a deck of cards and dealt them face up on the table from left to right in four rows of four cards each—i.e., in the order shown by the numbers below. From the following clues, can you correctly locate each of the cards?

(Note: "Row" denotes horizontal, "column" vertical.)

1. All of the aces are on the periphery of the arrangement.

2. The four corner cards, in no particular order, are the jack of hearts, the jack of clubs, the queen of diamonds, and the ace of clubs.

3. Each row and each column includes one card of each suit.

4. Each column includes one of each face card and one ace.

5. The second row has no aces in it.

6. The first card dealt was a club.

7. The queen of diamonds is not in the first row.

8. Card 12 is not a diamond.

9. Card 2 is not a spade.

10. The king of clubs was dealt after the queen of clubs.

The solution is on page 161.

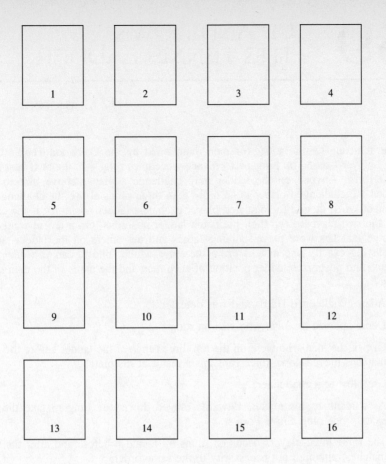

59

UP AND DOWN
THE TENNIS LADDER

by Margaret E. Shoop

On the ten-rung tennis ladder for men maintained by the Oakwood Tennis Club, the "best" player—based on prior performance—occupies rung #1, the next best rung #2, and so forth. Anyone on the ladder may challenge a player above him to a match provided the challenged player is no more than three rungs above the challenger. If the challenger wins, he and the defeated player exchange ladder positions; if the challenger loses, the two players keep their prematch ladder positions. On a recent weekend, five challenge matches were played among James and the others on the ladder, with each man playing exactly one match. From the clues which follow, can you determine the prematch and postmatch ladder position of each man and the name of the man he played against?

1. Adams challenged Harris and was defeated.

2. Dennis played the man who was on rung 7.

3. One of the men who were on the top three rungs of the ladder before the weekend matches moved down three rungs as a result of his match.

4. Grey lost to a challenger.

5. As a result of his match, Edwards moved down one rung to take the position exactly one rung above Forrest.

6. The same three players occupied rungs 6, 7, and 8 before and after the weekend matches, although not necessarily in the same order.

7. The same man was #4 on the ladder before and after his match.

8. The player on rung 3 didn't challenge the player on rung 1.

9. Brown, whose match was with Case, moved from at least one rung above Adams to at least one rung below him.

10. Kane was a losing challenger.

The solution is on page 162.

	PREMATCH	POSTMATCH
#1	_____	_____
#2	_____	_____
#3	_____	_____
#4	_____	_____
#5	_____	_____
#6	_____	_____
#7	_____	_____
#8	_____	_____
#9	_____	_____
#10	_____	_____

60 FATHER'S DAY SHIRTS

by Nancy R. Patterson

For Father's Day, Colin and each of four other fathers received a white shirt from his child. Mary, Jim, and the other three children all selected the correct sizes. The collars of the five shirts measured 14½, 15, 15½, 16, and 16½ inches. One shirt was short-sleeved (less than 12 inches long); the sleeve lengths of the other four were either 32, 33, or 34 inches. From the clues below, can you deduce each father's full name (one surname is Schick), his child's name, and the neck size and sleeve length of the shirt he received?

1. The shirt with French cuffs, given by a girl, had the same sleeve length as the shirt given by one of the boys; no other two measurements were the same.

2. The shirt Billy gave his father measured one inch longer in the sleeve than the one the Larson boy gave his father, but it was smaller in the collar.

3. Gil's collar size is an inch and a half larger than Mr. Powell's.

4. Mr. Malone was given a longer sleeve than the man who received the shirt with French cuffs.

5. Linda's father does not wear the largest collar.

6. Nick isn't the father who received the short-sleeved shirt.

7. Emily's gift was one inch larger in the collar than the Harris boy's.

8. The shirt with the 16-inch collar had a 33-inch sleeve.

9. Ted's son isn't the boy who gave the shirt with a 15½-inch collar.

10. Kevin's child is a boy.

Use the divided chart in the regular way.

The solution is on page 162.

	Billy	Emily	Jim	Linda	Mary	Colin	Gil	Kevin	Nick	Ted	sleeve				
Harris															
Larson															
Malone															
Powell															
Schick															
14½															
15															
15½															
16															
16½															
sleeve															
Colin															
Gil															
Kevin															
Nick															
Ted															

	14½	15	15½	16	16½
Harris					
Larson					
Malone					
Powell					
Schick					

CHALLENGER LOGIC PROBLEMS

61 BRISTOL HIGH REUNION

by Roseann Fairchild

On the eve of the recent tenth reunion of a Bristol High School class, held at the school, the Franks hosted a patio party for four other couples who were also attending the event, including the Greens. To their surprise, they learned each person who came to the party had the same occupation as someone else, and each also shared a hobby with someone else, although no husband and wife shared either occupation or hobby. From the clues below, can you find each person's full name (one man is Ken and one woman Donna) and determine their occupations and avocations? (Among the group are two dentists, two amateur chefs, and two amateur golfers.)

1. At Bristol High, one of the bridge fans had dated the woman whose married surname is Frank, but he later married an attorney. Another man, who is now a teacher, had dated the other three women: Eve, a woman who became an artist, and a bridge player.

2. Two of the couples—the teacher and her husband and Neil and his wife—were staying with the Ians while visiting in Bristol.

3. Ozzie, who is not a lawyer, has often exchanged recipes with the wife of the physician, who is not Cheryl; both Ozzie and the physician's wife are Bristol residents.

4. Betsy, who did not attend Bristol High and does not live in Bristol, has the same occupation as Mr. Johnson.

5. Max, who married a jogger, is not the male tennis player.

6. The woman named Johnson and Lee, who are both Bristol residents, share both hobby and occupation, so they see each other frequently.

7. The man named Holt, who is not a Bristol High alumnus and did not attend college, met both Ann—with whom he has something in common—and the woman named Ian for the first time on this occasion.

8. Neither artist attended college.

The solution is on page 163.

The solution is on page 163.

	husband	occupation	avocation	wife	occupation	avocation
Frank						
Green						
Holt						
Ian						
Johnson						

62 THE JAYS

by Dodi Schultz

Sent to cover a concert by the sensational young musical aggregation known as the Jays, Patty Popart, the *Gazette*'s cultural affairs reporter, unfortunately ran into a traffic jam and arrived after the performance had ended. Patty knew only the names of the nine young musicians and the fact that their ages ranged from ten to sixteen. Reasoning that she at least had to find out each one's age and musical instrument, she rushed backstage and happily found that they hadn't yet left the concert hall. She confessed her problem, and the youngsters, who were fond of having a bit of fun at the expense of the press, proceeded, speaking in alphabetical order, to make a series of statements, as follows:

1. Jack said, "Jimmy is a year older than Jeffrey."

2. Jane said, "I play the piano and so does Jeremy, and Jack plays guitar."

3. Jeffrey said, "I'm the same age as Jimmy, and Joanne is three years older."

4. Jeremy said, "Joy is eleven, and Jack is a year younger than I am."

5. Jimmy said, "June plays piano."

6. Joanne said, "I'm thirteen, and only three of the others are older."

7. Johnny said, "I'm the same age as June."

8. Joy said, "Jane is twelve."

9. June said, "I play piano."

Patty, who had hastily recorded these statements, looked them over and found that she was hardly more enlightened than before. Some of the statements were clearly in conflict with others—and further, she had noticed instruments on the stage that had not been mentioned. She pleaded for more help, and five of the youngsters smilingly obliged, as follows:

10. Jane said, "I'm the oldest."

11. Jeffrey said, "Both June and I play violin."

12. Jeremy said, "Joanne and Joy both play drums."

13. Joanne said, "Johnny is twelve and plays the ukulele, and Jimmy plays guitar."

14. Johnny said, "Jeffrey plays violin and Jane plays piano."

Perplexed as ever, Patty frowned at the fourteen statements and shook her head. Just then, Gig Bigbucks, the group's manager, arrived to shepherd his charges to a late-night interview show. Advised of Patty's dilemma, he sighed, "Yes, they're at it again. And I've got to go along with them; it's in the contract. But I can give you two hints: The majority of them tell the truth; the others do not tell the truth. But, those who tell the truth always do, and those who don't tell the truth never tell the truth. And whatever they said about the instrument June plays, one and only one statement was true." With that, he and the group departed, leaving Patty to puzzle over her notes. And, to her amazement, it took her just a few minutes to figure out the age and instrument of every one of the Jays. Can you do the same? (*Note: The youngsters' ages were all whole numbers of years.*)

The solution is on page 164.

Use this space for solving.

63 ZODIAC PAIRS

by Haydon Calhoun

Six married couples (one of whom was named Richards) were spending the weekend together at Lake Lawakoni Lodge. During a discussion of birth dates, Ron and Doris, both avid astrology buffs, were amazed to find that they and the ten others were all born under different signs of the zodiac, and that, surprisingly enough, the three spring signs were married to the three winter signs, as were the summer signs to autumn signs—a rare coincidence indeed! Using the astrological chart to help you with the clues below, try to determine who is married to whom, their last names, and their birth signs.

1. Jack was born May 5th, while Rebecca was born in March, Ken and Mary in September.

2. On Saturday while their husbands were fishing, three of the women—Rachel, Mrs. Sanford, and the Capricorn—played cards in the air-conditioned comfort of the clubhouse; both Mrs. Fleming and the Scorpio spent the day on the beach, while the sixth woman, a nature-lover, went on a bird-watching walk in the nearby woods.

3. The six husbands caught plenty of bass for the evening's cookout: Mr. Hudson caught 12, Mr. Sanford 10, Donald and Ken 8 each, and David Yates 6. The Piscean, contrary to his lucky fish sign, caught only 4.

4. When it came time for each man to broil his own entire catch, the Aquarian's husband and the Libran's husband proved to be the best cooks. Of the four others, Joyce's husband cooked two fish more than Anna's husband, while Robert cooked six fewer than the Moon Child's husband.

5. While the men were cooking, Joyce and Mrs. Winston occupied themselves applying soothing lotion to the painfully burned backs of sunbathers Anna and Rebecca.

This chart, designed by the puzzle's constructor, is what we used to solve the Logic Problem. We suggest that you note by a sign whether that person is a man or a woman when you know that, even if you don't yet know the person's name. We found this to be very helpful.

The solution is on page 164.

TAURUS		GEMINI		MOON CHILDREN		LEO	
Apr 20–May 19		May 20–June 20		June 21– July 21		July 22–Aug 21	
The Bull	2	The Twins	3	4	The Crab	5	The Lion

ARIES — Mar 21–Apr 19 — The Ram — 1

PISCES — Feb 19–Mar 20 — The Fishes — 12

SPRING SUMMER AUTUMN WINTER

The Virgin — VIRGO — Aug 22–Sept 21 — 6

The Balance — LIBRA — Sept 22–Oct 22 — 7

The Water Bearer	11	The Goat	10	9	The Archer	8	The Scorpion
AQUARIUS		CAPRICORN		SAGITTARIUS		SCORPIO	
Jan 21–Feb 18		Dec 22–Jan 20		Nov 23–Dec 21		Oct 23–Nov 22	

64 AT THE SUPERMARKET

by Mary A. Powell

At the Windy City Supermarket, Ms. Lewis and seven other women waited in the express checkout lane. Each woman had five items, and each had chosen from among this list: tomatoes (by the can), peas (by the can), bread (by the loaf), milk (by the quart), lettuce (by the head), and onions (on a unit basis). From the following clues, can you determine the full name of each woman (two first names are Cheryl and Evelyn) and what she bought?

1. No two women had the same combination of purchases. Six of the women bought five different items; one bought four different kinds of items.

2. Francine bought no canned goods and no produce (lettuce and onions).

3. Helen, Ms. Davis, and the only woman whose first and last names begin with the same letter all bought no onions.

4. Ms. Bailey, who is married, bought no bread; Beatrice bought no milk.

5. Dana and two other women bought no tomatoes; Ms. Collins bought no onions; Gina bought no peas.

6. Ms. Ingersoll bought two cans of peas; Ms. Davis bought two quarts of milk.

7. Arlene and Ms. Graham are both single; Ms. Arnold and Ms. Edwards are married.

8. Beatrice, who is married, is not Ms. Arnold.

The solution is on page 165.

We suggest using either zero (0) or a number in the items-bought boxes of the chart.

	A.	B.	C.	D.	E.	F.	G.	H.	tomatoes	peas	bread	milk	lettuce	onions
Arnold														
Bailey														
Collins														
Davis														
Edwards														
Graham														
Ingersoll														
Lewis														
tomatoes								
peas								
bread								
milk								
lettuce								
onions								

65 THE COMPANY PICNIC

by Nancy R. Patterson

Everyone brought either a spouse or child(ren) or both to the company picnic.

Everyone whose spouse was present took part in the sack race. The men with no children present took part in the beer-drinking contest. All those who had any children present balanced peanuts on their noses in a relay race.

One prize was awarded in each contest: for the sack race, a bottle of beer; for the beer-drinking contest, a paper sack; for the peanut relay, a jar of peanut butter.

From the following facts about the three prize-winners, can you tell not only which contest each won, but also the sex of each and which family member(s) each brought?

1. The winners of the bottled beer and peanut butter were of opposite sexes.

2. Chris took part in more than one contest.

3. Lee wasn't in any contest Chris was in.

4. Pat had exactly as many family members present as Chris.

5. Each winner had a different combination of family members present. For example, if one winner had both a wife and child(ren) present, no other winner did—although another might have had a husband and child(ren) present.

The solution is on page 165.

Use this space for solving.

66 MISPLACED PLACE CARDS

by Julie Spence

Last week, Paula Truman and her husband gave a dinner party for four other married couples. Preparations for the party were taken care of by both Mr. and Mrs. Truman. One of the things Paula was in charge of was setting the table. Just before the guests were due to arrive, Paula realized she wouldn't have time to finish everything and asked her husband to help. "Here are the place cards," she said. "Start with mine at the north end of the table, put the next card at the setting to my left, and proceed around the table. You and I will be on the ends." Paula then left the dining room. Later, when everyone was sitting down to dinner, Paula noticed that not one person, not even her husband, was sitting where she had intended. After dinner, Mr. Truman confessed to his wife that he had dropped the place cards and, since he was not sure of the order, he had put them around as best he could. "I remembered you wanted to alternate men and women. I did that," he said. "Oh, more than that," Paula said, "you remembered to put us at the ends of the table, and you put everyone in a place where they had a great time!" From the information below, can you determine Mr. Truman's first name, the full names of the eight guests, where Paula had intended to seat everyone, and where they ended up? *Note: (1) The Trumans have a rectangular table seating one person at each end and four on each side. (2) You may assume all the wives have adopted their husbands' surnames. (3) "Next to" can refer to a person at the end and the person to his/her left or right.*

1. Paula had intended to put husbands on opposite sides of the table from their wives.

2. These four ended up on the west side of the table, in no particular order: the Millers, Mr. Brown, and Brenda.

3. Amy ended up between Jim and another man; neither was her husband, and neither was the host.

4. Paula had intended to place Ken and Mr. Rockford directly across from each other, and that is how they ended up.

5. Mr. Washburn ended up next to his wife.

6. Paula had not intended for John to sit next to Joan, and he did not end up next to her.

7. Paula had intended for these four to sit on the same side of the table: Mark, Mr. Brown, Nora, and Mrs. Miller.

8. The person Paula had intended for John's immediate left did not end up to his immediate left or right.

9. Paula had not intended for Bob to be across from her or to her immediate left or right.

The solution is on page 166.

INTENDED

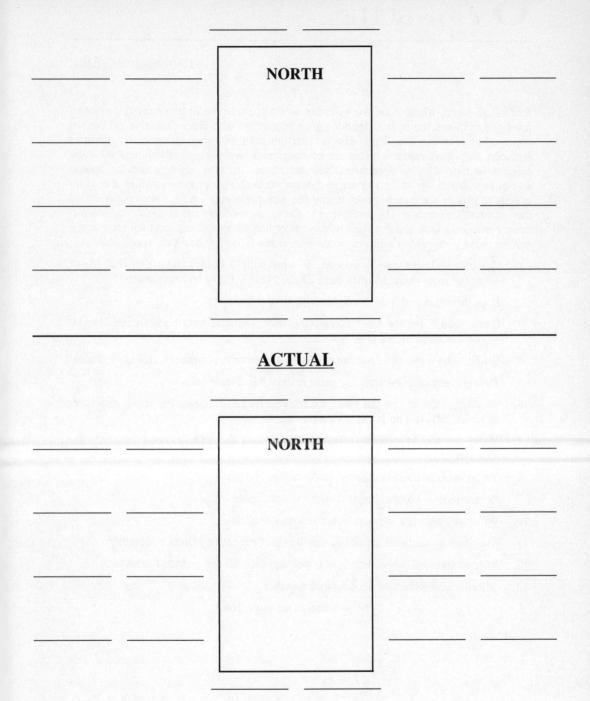

```
           _____  _____

_____  _____   ┌─────────────────┐   _____  _____
                         │                 │
                         │      NORTH       │
                         │                 │
_____  _____   │                 │   _____  _____
                         │                 │
                         │                 │
                         │                 │
_____  _____   │                 │   _____  _____
                         │                 │
                         │                 │
                         │                 │
_____  _____   │                 │   _____  _____
                         │                 │
                         └─────────────────┘
           _____  _____
```

ACTUAL

```
           _____  _____

_____  _____   ┌─────────────────┐   _____  _____
                         │                 │
                         │      NORTH       │
                         │                 │
                         │                 │
                         │                 │
                         │                 │
_____  _____   │                 │   _____  _____
                         │                 │
                         │                 │
                         │                 │
_____  _____   │                 │   _____  _____
                         │                 │
                         │                 │
                         │                 │
_____  _____   │                 │   _____  _____
                         └─────────────────┘
           _____  _____
```

119

67 EXECUTIVE SUITE

by Dodi Schultz

At Stiff & Stern, where Alan works either as a top executive or as secretary to one of the top executives, there is a definite office hierarchy. The chief executive officer, of course, outranks the president, who in turn outranks all other officers; the treasurer outranks the vice-presidents (who are of equal rank with one another), and all these officers outrank all their secretaries. The secretaries, in turn, enjoy a ranking among themselves based on their respective bosses' ranks. For example, while the chief executive officer's secretary ranks below the vice-presidents', he (or she) ranks above the president's secretary. The secretaries to the vice-presidents are of equal (and lowest) rank. From these facts and the clues below concerning six executives and their secretaries, can you give each person's full name (one surname is Upton) and exact position?

1. Grace ranks lower than Townsend, on a par with O'Reilly, and higher than Iris or John; the latter outranks only three of the twelve, Barry and two others.

2. Both Whitman and Van Buren outrank John.

3. Larry, who is not the chief executive officer, outranks both Kathryn and Harold, whose last name is not O'Reilly.

4. Quinn, who is the chief executive officer's secretary, is neither Carol nor Frances.

5. Two of the vice-presidents are men; neither has a male secretary.

6. Shaeffer, who is not the chief executive officer, outranks Patterson; the latter outranks David, who is not a vice-president.

7. Markham, a male secretary who outranks at least one other, is not secretary to the treasurer.

8. Yarborough, who is not Barry, ranks below Norton.

9. Robinson is a woman; her first name is not Frances.

10. Whitman, who is a woman, ranks below Patterson.

11. Evelyn, who outranks David, is not the chief executive officer's secretary.

12. At least three of the secretaries are women; they do not include Kathryn.

13. O'Reilly and Robinson do not work together.

The solution is on page 166.

Chief	_____ _____	Sec.	_____ _____
Pres.	_____ _____	Sec.	_____ _____
Treas.	_____ _____	Sec.	_____ _____
V-P	_____ _____	Sec.	_____ _____
V-P	_____ _____	Sec.	_____ _____
V-P	_____ _____	Sec.	_____ _____

68 CIRCUS SIDESHOWS

by Randall L. Whipkey

When the Dingling Brothers Circus made its annual appearance in Cozy Valley, six young couples decided to go to the show together. When they arrived at the Big Top lot, they found they were two hours early for the main performance, which was due to start at 3:00, so they decided to see the sideshows offered on the midway. The six sideshows each had performances scheduled one-half hour apart, at 1:00, 1:30, 2:00, and 2:30, so that the couples could not see all six attractions. When they found they couldn't agree on which four sideshows to see, the couples decided to go their separate ways, with each couple attending the four sideshows it preferred. Oddly, at each performance no two couples saw the same show, each viewing a different attraction at each of the four times. From the following clues, can you determine who dated whom and which sideshow each couple saw at each of the four performance times?

1. Barry and his date saw Azbesto the Fire Eater at the same time as Tom and his date saw Brobdingnag the Tallest Man, Sue and her date saw Zoro the Sword Swallower, and Jenny and her date saw Hercule the Strong Man.

2. Eddie and his date watched Medusa the Snake Charmer's act at the same time Linda and her date were seeing Illustro the Tattooed Man, Ralph and his date were seeing Azbesto, and Kim and her date were watching Brobdingnag.

3. Dick and his date saw Illustro at one of the first three performances.

4. Carol and her date particularly enjoyed Medusa's act; Jenny has a phobia about snakes, so she and her date bypassed the Snake Charmer's show, as did Tom and his date.

5. Two couples, Barry and his date and Kim and her date, did not see Hercule's performance.

6. At the same time as Ralph and his date saw Zoro, Tom and his date saw Hercule, Eddie and his date saw Azbesto, Sue and her date saw Medusa, and Kim and her date saw Illustro.

7. Ralph and his date saw Brobdingnag at an earlier show than Dick and his date did.

8. Kim and her date, who was not Frank, saw Zoro's act.

9. Eddie and his date watched Medusa's performance at an earlier show than Frank and his date.

10. Barry and his date saw Azbesto's act at the show immediately following the one at which Alice and her date saw him.

The solution is on page 167.

PERFORMANCES ATTENDED

couples	1:00	1:30	2:00	2:30

69

SCHEDULES FOR SUBSTITUTES

by Evelyn B. Rosenthal

There are six math teachers at Central High School, which encompasses grades eight through twelve; each teaches five classes in the seven-period day. Since the school has no provision for hiring substitutes, each is responsible for filling in during a different preassigned period (one of the teacher's two free ones) in case a colleague who is supposed to teach that period is absent. In the math department schedule, all sections of a grade meet at the same time; that is, one period is devoted only to eighth-grade math classes, one to ninth-grade (freshman) classes, one to tenth (sophomore), eleventh (junior), and twelfth (senior) classes. There are not necessarily the same number of sections in each grade. One of the remaining two periods is reserved for remedial classes, and some special-interest classes meet in the other. From the following clues, can you determine the department's daily schedule and each teacher's individual program?

1. Harris is the substitute for first-period classes; neither Jones nor Smith is available then.

2. Three of the teachers could act as substitutes in the senior class; Gerson is the one with that assignment.

3. Gerson and Karp could trade their substitute assignments.

4. Smith is the assigned substitute for the sophomore classes; neither Brown nor Harris is available for that assignment.

5. Karp is the substitute for the third-period classes.

6. Jones is the substitute for the fifth-period classes; neither Harris nor Smith is available then.

7. Brown is the substitute for the freshman classes, although he could have been assigned to second-period classes instead; neither Harris nor Smith is available as a substitute for the freshman classes.

8. No substitute is assigned to the seventh-period classes, since the two teachers who are free then have other substitute assignments, one in the fourth period and the other for the eighth-grade classes.

9. Jones could have been assigned to the remedial classes as substitute.

10. The classes meeting in the special-interest period are two in college math and two in computer science.

The solution is on page 168.

periods		teacher assignments					
No.	activity	Brown	Gerson	Harris	Jones	Karp	Smith
1st							
2nd							
3rd							
4th							
5th							
6th							
7th							

70 GROCERY SHOPPING

by Julie Spence

One recent Saturday morning, the checkout attendant at Lanie's Supermarket waited on twelve married couples consecutively. The interesting thing about this particular morning is that while waiting on these couples, the attendant checked out only six different grocery items: milk, orange juice, bread, cereal, eggs, and bacon; and he checked out exactly eight of each item, i.e., eight cartons of milk, eight dozen eggs, eight boxes of cereal, etc. Each husband and wife were waited on together and each couple bought the same number of items. But no two couples bought the same combination of items, and none of the couples bought two or more of the same item. From the information below, can you determine the full name of each husband and wife (one husband is Bob, one wife is Amy, and one surname is Wicker), in what order the couples were waited on, and what items each couple bought?

1. The Vandells, who bought bacon, were waited on before the Clarks, who were not waited on last.

2. The Thompsons bought milk, bread, bacon, and eggs.

3. The couples waited on 8th and 10th bought orange juice.

4. These five couples were waited on consecutively: the Bakers, Gary and his wife, a couple who bought orange juice and bacon, the Stevenses, and Bill and his wife.

5. Sue and her husband did not buy either bacon or eggs.

6. The couple who were waited on last did not buy cereal.

7. One of the items Tom and his wife bought was orange juice.

8. The Macks did not buy bread or cereal.

9. Fern and her husband bought milk, but not bread.

10. These five couples were waited on consecutively: Janet and her husband; Jack and his wife; the couple who bought milk, bread, orange juice, and bacon; the couple who did not buy either cereal or orange juice; and Jill and her husband.

11. The first five couples waited on all bought bread.

12. Chuck and his wife did not buy milk.

13. The couples waited on first, second, and fourth did not buy eggs.

14. Mary and her husband did not buy bread.

15. Neither Allen and his wife, who did not buy bacon, nor the Smiths bought milk.

16. Sally and her husband, who were not waited on tenth or twelfth, and John and his wife are two couples who bought both bacon and eggs.

17. The Nelsons, who did not buy milk or eggs, were waited on ninth.

18. Adam and his wife, who did not buy bacon, were waited on immediately before the Johnsons.

19. Steve and his wife bought cereal, orange juice, eggs, and one other item.

20. The last three couples waited on did not buy milk.

21. The Ameses did not buy eggs.

126

22. Judy and her husband bought cereal.

23. George and his wife bought eggs.

24. The four couples who did not buy milk are, in no particular order: Nola and her husband; the Vandells; Joe and his wife; and Diane and her husband (who did not buy eggs).

25. The Olsons bought both bread and eggs.

26. Carol and her husband, who did not buy eggs, were waited on immediately before Nikki and her husband.

The solution is on page 169.

	wife	husband	surname	bought
1st				
2nd				
3rd				
4th				
5th				
6th				
7th				
8th				
9th				
10th				
11th				
12th				

71 REIGNING CATS AND DOGS

by Haydon Calhoun

In Catdog Town's First and Last Annual Black and White Cat and Dog Show, pets were crowned "Best in Show" in twelve categories: black male and female cat and dog, white male and female cat and dog, black-and-white spotted male and female cat and dog. (Their owners were "purrfectly doglighted" with the results of the judging, but the pets were dog-tired, and a few took catnaps during the day-long proceedings.) Each winner already had an aristocratic name accurately reflecting its gender: Baron, Baroness, Count, Countess, Duke, Duchess, Emperor, Empress, King, Queen, Prince, or Princess. As it happens, there were also six males (Bob, Dane, Rex, Tab, Tom, and Wolf) and six females (Cathy, Chita, Kate, Kathy, Kit, and Kitty) among the winners' owners, although a pet's and owner's gender may or may not match. The last names of the twelve owners, not necessarily respectively, are Barker, Chow, Doggy, Felix, Fox, Katz, Lynx, Lyon, Manx, Mews, Setter, and Wolfe. From the following clues, can you (doggedly and without "paws," of course) find each owner's full name and the kind, color, and name of his or her pet?

1. Chita, Setter, Tom, and Wolf own the black pets.
2. Bob, Cathy, Kitty, and Mr. Doggy own the white pets.
3. Felix, Kate, Rex, and Tab own the spotted pets.
4. Only one owner, whose pet is Empress, has a first and last name beginning with the same letter.
5. Kate is not Lynx and Kathy is not Setter, but both Kate and Kathy own cats.
6. Kate, Katz, and Kit don't own King, but King's owner does have either a first or last name that begins with the same letter as his or her pet's name.
7. Chow is not Tom; Bob is not Lyon.
8. Rex has the same kind and gender pet as Kitty.
9. Kate, Kitty, and Tab have last names that end with identical letters.
10. Mr. Manx owns a male animal.
11. Only Rex and Ms. Wolfe have last names that end with the same letter as the first or last letter of their pets' names.
12. Count is a cat; Cathy owns a cat, but Chita doesn't.
13. Duke is a dog, but Duchess isn't; both are spotted.
14. Either Tab or Tom owns Duke; the other has a cat.
15. Baron, Baroness, and Prince are white.
16. Princess and Queen are black.
17. Both Baron's and Count's owners have surnames beginning with the same letters as their pets' names.

The solution is on page 170.

pet	cat	dog	color			owner
			bl.	wh.	sp.	
Baron						
Baroness						
Count						
Countess						
Duke						
Duchess						
Emperor						
Empress						
King						
Queen						
Prince						
Princess						

	Bob	Dane	Rex	Tab	Tom	Wolf	Cathy	Chita	Kate	Kathy	Kit	Kitty	cat	dog
Barker														
Chow														
Doggy														
Felix														
Fox														
Katz														
Lynx														
Lyon														
Manx														
Mews														
Setter														
Wolfe														
cat														
dog														

72 THE NINE MUSES

by Nancy R. Patterson

At a performance of an original ballet, *The Muses,* Mme. Delphic of the Delphic Dance Company arranged Ingrid and the other eight dancers in the following tableau for curtain calls: stage left, a principal dancer between two attendants; downstage center, the premiere danseuse in the role of Terpsichore, between two attendants; stage right, the third principal between two attendants. Madame assigned the dancers numbers from one (farthest left as we look at the stage from the audience) through nine (farthest right), the principals being two, five, and eight. After the first curtain call, dancers one and nine were to leave by the side exits, then—"Quickly, please!"—dancers two and eight, then—"Do hurry!"—dancers three and seven, leaving the downstage group to take the second call. In the event of a third curtain call, dancers four and six were to leave Terpsichore alone on the stage. Using our printed program to refresh your memory of the muses, you need only the clues below to complete the program with each dancer's full name (one last name is Quinn) and her curtain-call number.

1. In one group, "tragedy" (played by Ms. Rush) and "comedy" attended Kathy; in another, June as "epic poetry" and Ms. Stone as "lyric poetry" attended Bonnie; and in the third, Ms. Lyman stood between "religious music" and Gwen.

2. Fran White and Euterpe left the stage together; theirs was not the last exit.

3. Dancer 3 did not perform Melpomene.

4. Holly and Ms. Vass would have left the stage together if there'd been another curtain call.

5. Ms. Norton (who didn't portray Clio) exited after Ms. O'Hara and did not exit at the same time as Dana.

6. Ms. Young and Alice left the stage simultaneously; neither was Urania.

7. If a line had been drawn down the exact center of the stage, from back to front, Calliope would have been on one side of that line and Clio on the other.

DELPHIC DANCE COMPANY
presents

THE MUSES

	Performed by	Place
Calliope, epic poetry	_____	_____
Clio, history	_____	_____
Erato, lyric poetry	_____	_____
Euterpe, secular music	_____	_____
Melpomene, tragedy	_____	_____
Polyhymnia, religious music	_____	_____
Terpsichore, dance	_____	_____
Thalia, comedy	_____	_____
Urania, astronomy	_____	_____

The solution is on page 170.

EXIT ① ② ③ ④ ⑤ ⑥ ⑦ ⑧ ⑨ EXIT

73 JOB INTERVIEWS

by Randall L. Whipkey

The Cozy Valley Teachers College placement office arranges interviews between graduating students and prospective employers. One day this past spring, five seniors had interviews with superintendents from five school districts: one was Dr. Evans. Each student met individually with each of the five superintendents; each of the latter interviewed different students at 9:00, 10:00, 11:00, 1:00, and 2:00. From the clues below, can you determine each future teacher's full name (one last name is Newman), his or her major subject, each superintendent's school district, and the complete interview schedule?

1. Ms. Owens's interview with Dr. Adams was two hours later than the biology major's.

2. Ian met with Dr. Barnes one hour after being interviewed by the superintendent from Autumnton.

3. Helen's last name isn't Keller.

4. Gloria met with Dr. Cramer an hour before her interview with the Fallriver superintendent.

5. John's major is chemistry.

6. Dr. Barnes interviewed Helen an hour before interviewing Ms. Mason.

7. The Summerset superintendent interviewed the French major in the morning.

8. Keller's interview with the Autumnton superintendent wasn't at 11:00.

9. Faith and Dr. Adams met at 2:00.

10. Gloria's 9:00 interview was not with Dr. Adams.

11. The mathematics major's 2:00 interview wasn't with the Winterhaven superintendent.

12. Faith's 1:00 appointment was not with Dr. Cramer.

13. Gloria and Dr. Davis met at 1:00.

14. The English major's interview with the Springdale superintendent was an hour before Long's.

15. Gloria isn't the biology major.

16. Dr. Adams isn't the Fallriver superintendent.

The solution is on page 171.

	Adams of ————	Barnes of ————	Cramer of ————	Davis of ————	Evans of ————
9:00					
10:00					
11:00					
1:00					
2:00					

	Faith	Gloria	Helen	Ian	John	bio.	chem.	Eng.	Fr.	math
Keller										
Long										
Mason										
Newman										
Owens										
bio.					
chem.					
Eng.					
Fr.					
math					

74 AT THE FOOTBALL GAME

by Mary A. Powell

At a recent Jamison High School football game, the Jackson child, the Rider child, and the other 18 students in their class were assigned the 20 seats diagrammed on the next page. Seats 101 through 105 are the front row, with 201 through 205 behind them, and so on. From the following clues, can you give the students' full names and tell exactly where each sat?

1. The first and last names of one student who sat in the front row begin with the same letter.

2. Pamela and the Queen girl sat as far apart as possible; the same was true of the Connors boy and Ann.

3. The Davis girl sat directly (but not necessarily immediately) behind Ted, who sat immediately behind the Long girl.

4. These four students were in the same row: the Andrews girl, the Boyd boy, Ted, and Jane.

5. Carl sat immediately behind the Wilson girl.

6. Ned and the Landry girl sat at opposite ends of one row; Pamela and the Fowler girl sat at opposite ends of another row.

7. The Owens boy sat immediately in front of George and immediately behind the Egan girl, who sat immediately behind Will.

8. A boy sat in seat 403.

9. Beth sat between two boys; Bill sat between two girls.

10. The Connors boy sat directly (but not necessarily immediately) in front of the Holland boy, who sat immediately in front of Pamela.

11. Larry, Mary, Sandra, and the Morris boy were in the same row.

12. Diane had wanted to sit with David, but her row was two rows behind his.

13. Larry was not in seat 105.

14. Louise Landry sat two seats directly behind Mary.

15. The Smith boy and the Thompson girl sat in the same row, which was two rows behind the Iverson girl's.

16. Roger was in seat 103.

17. Jane sat immediately in front of a boy; Vicky was not in seat 205.

18. The Potter boy sat immediately behind Ted.

19. Frank is not the Owens boy; Carl's last name is not Allen.

20. The Allen boy sat two seats directly behind Karen.

The solution is on page 172.

401	402	403	404	405
301	302	303	304	305
201	202	203	204	205
101	102	103	104	105

75 HOUSEHOLD ORGANIZATION

by Virginia C. McCarthy

Mrs. Mintz and four other housewives recently decided to schedule their household chores so as to allow themselves relatively free weekends. Working together, they then broke down their housework into five categories: cooking, cleaning, laundry, shopping, and miscellaneous chores (mending, ironing, etc.); then each woman mapped out a weekly schedule whereby she assigned herself one chore per day for Mondays through Fridays. From the following clues, can you find the full names of the five women and reconstruct their weekly housework schedules?

1. On every day of their work week, one woman does her cleaning and another woman does her laundry.

2. Fanny does her laundry earlier in the week than Mrs. Pligh does her shopping and later in the week than Betty does her cleaning.

3. Mrs. Sayles has scheduled her weekly laundry, miscellaneous chores, and cooking in the order given—but not on three consecutive days.

4. Debbie and Mrs. Schein both do their shopping on the same day of the week.

5. Both Connie and Mrs. Rintz do their cleaning earlier in the week than Wednesday.

6. Three of the women do miscellaneous chores on Fridays; none of the five shops on Tuesdays.

7. Betty and Ellie do their cooking on Mondays and Tuesdays, respectively.

The solution is on page 173.

The solution is on page 173.

names	Monday	Tuesday	Wednesday	Thursday	Friday

	Betty	Connie	Debbie	Ellie	Fanny
Mintz					
Pligh					
Rintz					
Sayles					
Schein					

SOLUTIONS

1. THE DANCE CONTEST

The couple who fox-trotted won $40 and the couple who polkaed $20 (clue 4). The couples who tangoed and jitterbugged didn't win $10 (clue 1), so the waltzers did. The couple who tangoed didn't win $30 (clue 2), so the jitterbuggers did, and the tangoers won $50. By clue 4, Stan did the tango, Linda the jitterbug, and Thad the waltz. Neither Victor (clue 1) nor Warren (clue 2) jitterbugged, so Roger did and was Linda's partner. Victor didn't polka (clue 3), so Warren did, and Victor did the fox trot. By clue 1, since all five couples are mentioned, Jane's partner was not Thad, who won $10, or Stan, who tangoed, so Jane must have been Warren's partner. Since Karen wasn't Stan's (clue 2) or Victor's partner (clue 3), she must have been Thad's. Since Stan tangoed, his partner wasn't Harriet (clue 2), so she was Inez, and Harriet did the fox trot with Victor. In summary:

> Stan & Inez, tango, $50
> Victor & Harriet, fox trot, $40
> Roger & Linda, jitterbug, $30
> Warren & Jane, polka, $20
> Thad & Karen, waltz, $10

2. LAS VEGAS WEEKEND

Eric stayed at the Sun (clue 5). Max Blum, who saw the show at the Star (clue 2), did not stay at the Moon (clue 1), so he and his wife stayed at the Star—and his wife must be Mae (clue 3). Charles and Grace Brown also stayed at the Star (clue 6); therefore John and his wife stayed at the Moon, and saw the show at Nero's Castle (clue 1). The Steels saw the show at the Hill (clue 4), so Sarah Steel is not John's wife, and must be Eric's. John's wife is thus Irene, their last name Jones. By elimination, it was the Browns who saw the show at the Moon. In summary:

> Charles and Grace Brown stayed at Star, saw Moon show.
> Max and Mae Blum stayed at Star, saw Star show.
> John and Irene Jones stayed at Moon, saw Nero's Castle show.
> Eric and Sarah Steel stayed at Sun, saw Hill show.

3. THE GOLDEN-AGERS

Neither Jenny (clue 1), Sarah (clue 2), nor Susan (clue 4), is either the oldest or youngest, and Anna is not the oldest (clue 5); Louise is thus the oldest, Anna the youngest. The women's ages, as stated, may range from 91 to 99, inclusive. By clue 3, the ages of four must be 92, 94, 96, and 98. Anna cannot be 91, since that would require another odd-numbered age in the group (clue 5), so she is 92. She is not Mrs. Bowen (clues 1, 2), Mrs. King, or Mrs. Walker (clue 5), nor can she be the odd-number aged Mrs. Wall (clue 3), so she is Mrs. Jones. Thus, by clue 5, Mrs. King must be 94, and Mrs. Walker 96; Mrs. Bowen must be Louise, 98. Jenny, then, is 95 (clue 1), and is Mrs. Wall (clue 3). Sarah is Mrs. King (clue 2); Susan, by elimination, is Mrs. Walker. In summary, the five and their ages are:

> Anna Jones, 92
> Sarah King, 94
> Jenny Wall, 95
> Susan Walker, 96
> Louise Bowen, 98

4. FOOTBALL GAME WATCHERS

Jean and Anderson were still watching the game after Jenkins had gone home, and all three are Warriors fans (clues 4 and 5). The fourth person, Hugh, is a Braves fan (clue 2). Jenkins, being a guest, (clue 4) is not Mike, so Anderson must be Mike, and Jenkins is Donna. Hugh's last name isn't Horner (clue 2), so it must be Blakely, and Jean's last name is Horner. The building contractor isn't Donna or Mike (clue 1), or Jean Horner (clue 7), and thus must be Hugh Blakely. The programmer, who was the last guest to leave (clue 6), cannot be Mike, the host, or Donna Jenkins, who left early (clue 4); the programmer thus must be Jean Horner. Donna isn't the dentist (clue 3), so Mike is, and Donna is the statistician. In summary:

> Mike Anderson, dentist
> Hugh Blakely, building contractor
> Jean Horner, programmer
> Donna Jenkins, statistician

5. THE CRAFT FAIR

From clue 5, we know that the six are: the potter; Kay; Joan; the jewelry maker; the woman who does patchwork; and Olivia. Peter is not the potter (clue 2), nor can he be the woman who does patchwork, so he makes jewelry. Marge does not do patchwork (clue 3), so she is the potter, and Laura, by elimination, does patchwork. Neither Kay (clue 1) nor Joan (clue 4) is the weaver, so Olivia is. Joan is not the woodcarver (clue 4), so Kay is, and Joan is the glassblower. Kay's one exchange of wares was not with Olivia, who arranged no trades at all (clue 5), so it was with Laura (clue 1). From clue 5, then, Marge made two trades, one with Joan and again with Peter. In summary:

> Kay (woodcarving) traded with Laura (patchwork).
> Marge (pottery) traded with Peter (jewelry) and Joan (glassblowing).
> Olivia (weaving) did no trading.

6. DOCTORS' VISITS

We are told that one patient is Jack, and a second is Jim Fisk (clue 1). The other three women are: Dr. Noble's patient, Ms. Falmer, and the one who saw the dermatologist (clue 2). Dr. Noble must be Ms. Foster's surgeon (clue 3). Jill Furness (clue 7) is therefore the one who saw the dermatologist. Jack's surname, by elimination, is French. The woman who went to the obstetrician, who is not Janet (clue 6), must be Jean Falmer. Janet, by elimination, is Ms. Foster. The woman who went to Dr. Aronson is not Jean (clue 5), so she is Jill. The orthopedist isn't Jack French's doctor (clue 4) and must be Jim Fisk's, while Jack saw the ophthalmologist. Dr. Carter isn't the orthopedist (also clue 4) or the obstetrician (clue 6) and must be the ophthalmologist. Jim's doctor is not Dr. Pershy (clue 1) and must be Dr. Sands, while Dr. Pershy is Jean's doctor. In summary:

> Jean Falmer: obstetrician Pershy
> Jim Fisk: orthopedist Sands
> Janet Foster: surgeon Noble
> Jack French: ophthalmologist Carter
> Jill Furness: dermatologist Aronson

7. THE VACATIONERS

Neither the Joneses (clue 1), the Johnsons (clue 5), nor the Wilsons (clue 6) traveled by van or pickup camper; the Aldriches did not travel by pickup camper (clue 3), so the Harrisons did, and the Aldriches traveled by van. Neither couple visited Yellowstone (clue 1), Alaska (clue 2), or Oregon (clues 3, 4). The Aldriches did not visit New England (clue 4), so the Harrisons did, and the Aldriches visited Canada. The Joneses did not go to Alaska or Yellowstone (clue 1), so they went to the Oregon mountains. The Johnsons did not go to Alaska (clue 5), so the Wilsons did, and the Johnsons visited Yellowstone. Neither the Joneses nor the Johnsons took a cruise (clue 7), and the Johnsons did not go backpacking (also clue 7), so the Wilsons took the cruise to Alaska, the Johnsons went camping in Yellowstone, and the Joneses went backpacking in Oregon. In summary:

> Aldriches: Canada, van
> Harrisons: New England, pickup camper
> Johnsons: Yellowstone, camping
> Joneses: Oregon, backpacking
> Wilsons: Alaska, cruise

8.   THE DEFUNCT-CAR CLUB

Neither the Nike (clue 6), Kratos (clue 3), Pegasus (clue 4), or Sibyl (clue 5) is the oldest car, so the Hydra is. The Nike isn't the '55 model (clue 2), and it is newer than two others in addition to the Hydra (clue 6), so it's the '53 model. The Kratos thus is the '49 model (clue 6), George's car a '51 (also clue 6), and Mark's the '55 model (clue 2). Since Conway's car is older than the Kratos (clue 3), he owns the '47 Hydra. In clue 1, then, since the cars mentioned are the three oldest and George owns the '51, Conway must be James, and Brooks owns the '49 Kratos. Since Andrews's car is neither the '53 nor the '55 (clue 5), he must own one of the three oldest cars and must thus be George; George Andrews does not own the Sibyl (clue 5). He therefore owns the Pegasus, leaving the Sibyl to be the '55 model, owned by Mark. Harry thus owns the '49 Kratos (clue 4). By elimination, Larry owns the Nike. Davis doesn't own the Sibyl (clue 5), so he owns the Nike and is Larry. Mark East owns the Sibyl. In summary:

> James Conway, '47 Hydra
> Harry Brooks, '49 Kratos
> George Andrews, '51 Pegasus
> Larry Davis, '53 Nike
> Mark East, '55 Sibyl

9.   LEARNING A TRADE

Since Dan did not work for the mechanic (clue 2), he is his son. From clue 1, Ted worked for the electrician in July, so he is not his son; he is the carpenter's son, and Abe, for whom he worked in August, must be the mechanic. Mr. White is not the mechanic or the carpenter (clue 3), so he is the electrician Ted worked for in July. Abe, Dan's father, is not Mr. Brown (clue 2), so he is Mr. Green, and Mr. Brown is the carpenter. Dan must have worked for Mr. Brown in July and for Mr. White in August. Hal's last name must be White (clue 4), and he worked for Mr. Green in July and for Mr. Brown in August. The latter is not Joe (also clue 4), so Mr. White is, and Mr. Brown, by elimination, is Bud. In summary:

> Carpenter Bud Brown: son, Ted; July, Dan; Aug., Hal
> Mechanic Abe Green: son, Dan; July, Hal; Aug., Ted
> Electrician Joe White: son, Hal; July, Ted; Aug., Dan

10.   THE WILDLIFE WALK

Since the hike proceeded northward, Daisy spotted the first animal on the southernmost farm (clue 3). Bear Creek does not touch the two northernmost farms, so Jill's was the second or third sighting (clue 2), as was that of the skunk spotted by one of the boys (clue 9). Thus, from clue 6, Ellen spotted her animal on the fourth property, the Arden farm; the skunk was the third animal sighted; and Jill's sighting was the second. The first and last properties visited were not the Moore farm (clue 1) or the Brooks farm (clue 4), so they were in one order or the other the Crane and Noble farms; by clue 7, then, the Noble farm is the southernmost and the Crane farm the northernmost. The Brooks farm is south of the one where a fox was seen running from a red barn (clue 4)—in fact, immediately south of it (clue 8), so the Brooks farm is where the skunk was

141

seen, and Ellen spotted the fox. Jill's sighting, by elimination, was at the Moore farm. The deer was not sighted by Jill (clue 2) or Daisy (clues 3, 5), so it was the last animal seen. Nor did Jill spot the rabbit (clue 1), so Daisy did, and Jill sighted the squirrel. Will sighted the deer and Carl the skunk (clue 4). In summary, from south to north:

> Noble: Daisy, rabbit
> Moore: Jill, squirrel
> Brooks: Carl, skunk
> Arden: Ellen, fox
> Crane: Will, deer

11. NIGHT ON THE TOWN

Edwina was escorted by Mr. Black (clue 1), so his first name is not Edwin. Nor is it Henry (also clue 1) or Robert (clue 3), so it is Alvin. He is not the corporation President (clue 1), the Treasurer (clue 2), or the Vice-President (clue 3), so he is the Secretary. Henry is not the President (clue 1). Since Edwina and Alvin Black did not arrive at the supper club first or last (clue 1) or second (clue 3), they were the third couple to arrive. Thus, by the same two clues, Henry was the last corporation officer to arrive, his secretary is Miss Brown, and he cannot be the Vice-President; he must be the Treasurer, and Miss Brown's first name is Alvina (clue 2). Henry's last name is White (clue 3). Edwin is not the Vice-President (clue 3), so he is the President, and the Vice-President is Robert. Since the latter's secretary cannot be Roberta, she must be Henrietta, and Roberta is Edwin's secretary. Edwin's last name is either Brown or Gold. Since Miss Brown is the Treasurer's secretary, Edwin's surname is Gold (clue 3); thus Robert's secretary is Henrietta Gold, and Robert's last name is Brown. Edwina's surname is not Black, so it is White, and Miss Black is Roberta. In summary, the four officers and their secretaries are:

> President Edwin Gold—Roberta Black
> Vice-President Robert Brown—Henrietta Gold
> Secretary Alvin Black—Edwina White
> Treasurer Henry White—Alvina Brown

12. THE NEIGHBORHOOD CHILDREN

From clue 1, Mrs. Gray, who has more than one child, goes to work every Saturday afternoon, while Mrs. White, who has a daughter, is always home on Saturday afternoons. Clue 4 describes two other women—Rita's mother, who is sometimes home on Saturday afternoons (and thus cannot be either Mrs. Gray or Mrs. White), and Gary's mother, who sometimes shops on Saturday afternoons (and thus, by the same token, cannot be Mrs. Gray or Mrs. White). Since there are five children altogether, Mrs. Gray must have two children, and each of the other three mothers, one child; that is, the five children are the two Gray children, the White girl, Rita, and Gary. Gary's last name is not Brown, since the Brown child is a girl (clue 3), so Gary is the Green child and Rita the Brown child. We are told that all the children are different ages, from three to seven. The three-year-old is not one of the Gray children (clue 1), Gary Green (clue 2), or Rita Brown (clue 3), so she must be the White girl; she is not Tina (clue 2), so she is Lisa. Rita Brown is then five years old (clue 3). From clue 2, then, Gary Green, Tina, and Larry must be, respectively, the seven-year-old, the six-year-old, and the four-year-old. Tina and Larry, by elimination, are the Gray children. In summary:

> Gary Green, 7
> Tina Gray, 6
> Rita Brown, 5
> Larry Gray, 4
> Lisa White, 3

13. HURRICANE IWA

Based on the information in the introduction, there are just six possible combinations of tree losses: mango-avocado, mango-papaya, mango-plumeria, palm-avocado, palm-papaya, and palm-plumeria. By clue 1, we know that each home lost a different one of the above combinations. The Elmores lost a palm and a plumeria (clue 5). The Ambroses lost a palm but not an avocado (clue 3), so the other tree they lost was a papaya. The Baldwins lost a mango (clue 4). The Ambroses' anemometer registered 103 (clue 3), the Baldwins' 98 (clue 4); since these were respectively the highest and lowest readings, the others were 99, 100, 101, and 102. A fourth family's anemometer registered 99, and that family lost a mango and a papaya (clue 7). By clue 6, since the Elmores' anemometer must have registered at least 100, the only possibility is that it did register 100, while the Cases' registered 101 and the Deans' 102. The anemometer registering 99, by elimination, was the Freemans', who lost the mango and papaya. We have accounted for both papayas and one plumeria. By clue 2, then, the second plumeria was the Deans', while both the Baldwins and the Cases lost avocados. Since the Baldwins' second loss was a mango, the Cases lost a palm. The Deans, by elimination, lost a mango. In summary:

> Ambrose: palm and papaya, 103
> Baldwin: mango and avocado, 98
> Case: palm and avocado, 101
> Dean: mango and plumeria, 102
> Elmore: palm and plumeria, 100
> Freeman: mango and papaya, 99

14. THE HAPPY DIETERS

Mrs. Nelson lost the most weight, Gloria the second most; Eva and Mrs. Miller lost the least (clue 3). Mrs. Nelson is not Fran (clue 1), so she is Helen. Fran did not lose the least (also clue 1), so she lost the next-to-least and must be Mrs. Miller. Eva then lost the least; she is not Mrs. Paulson (clue 2), so she is Mrs. Oliver, and Gloria is Mrs. Paulson, who lost 30 pounds (also clue 2). Gloria's husband is not Bill (clue 2) or Dave (clue 3). If he were Clyde, then Helen would have lost 40 pounds (clue 4) and be married to Art—but since Fran would then have lost at least 11 pounds less than Helen, that would be impossible (clue 1). So Gloria must be married to Art. Fran Miller then lost 22 pounds, and Eva Oliver lost 16 (clue 1). Since the total weight loss for the four women was 100 pounds, Helen Nelson must have lost 32 pounds. Fran's husband is then Clyde (clue 4). Bill must be Eva's husband (clue 2), and Dave is Mr. Nelson. In summary, the four couples with the amount of weight lost by each woman, ranked by amount lost, are:

> Helen (32 pounds) and Dave Nelson
> Gloria (30 pounds) and Art Paulson
> Fran (22 pounds) and Clyde Miller
> Eva (16 pounds) and Bill Oliver

15. A WHO-DONE-IT-FIRST MYSTERY

The villain who used the gun was fourth in appearance (clue 3). Peter Lorre was not first (clue 1), nor was Lon Chaney (clue 2), Boris Karloff or Sydney Greenstreet (clue 4); therefore, the villain who actually murdered the victim was Bela Lugosi. Bela did not use poison (clue 1), nor did he strangle the victim (clue 2), nor use the dagger (clue 5); he must have electrocuted him. Since Lon Chaney reached the victim before the strangler (clue 2), and Boris and Sydney arrived after the strangler (clue 4), the strangler was the third villain and Lon was the second. The strangler being the third villain, Boris must be the fourth (who used the gun) and Sydney the fifth and last (clue 4). Peter then is the strangler. Lon did not use the dagger (clue 5), so he must have tried the poison dart. Sydney, then, used the dagger. Sydney is not the gangster or the spy (clue 3), the smuggler (clue 6), or the maniac (clue 7), so he must be the forger. Boris, who used the gun, is not the spy or the gangster (clue 3), or the maniac (clue 7), so he is the smuggler. Peter is the maniac (clue 5). Bela then must be the gangster, since he arrived before the spy (clue 3), and the spy must be Lon Chaney. In summary, in order of their appearance:

143

Bela Lugosi, gangster, electric shock
Lon Chaney, spy, poison dart
Peter Lorre, maniac, strangling
Boris Karloff, smuggler, gun
Sydney Greenstreet, forger, dagger

16. THE IVY LEAGUERS

By clue 4, Vic and Ford, in one order or the other, must be the boxer and the equestrian. Ford is not the boxer (clue 2), so he is the equestrian, and Vic is the Princeton boxer (clue 6). Vic's last name is not Inman then (clue 1), Atkins (clue 2), Ford (clue 4), or Jacobs (clue 6); so Massey is Vic the Princeton boxer. Ford's first name is not Nat (clue 1), Kip, or Russ (clue 2); it is Ted. Inman's first name is not Nat (clue 1) or Russ (clue 3); it is Kip. Russ is not Atkins (clue 2), so he is Jacobs, and Nat is Atkins. By clue 1, the Cornell man is not Ford, Nat Atkins, or Inman; he is Jacobs. Kip Inman is not the Harvard sprinter (clue 3), the gymnast, or the Dartmouth man (clue 5), so he is the Yale weight lifter. Equestrian Ted Ford must then attend Dartmouth, while the gymnast is Jacobs, and Atkins is the Harvard sprinter. In summary:

Nat Atkins—Harvard sprinter
Ted Ford—Dartmouth equestrian
Kip Inman—Yale weight lifter
Russ Jacobs—Cornell gymnast
Vic Massey—Princeton boxer

17. THE PIZZA PARLOR

Neither mushroom nor sausage (clue 2), anchovy (clue 5), nor pepperoni (clue 6), pizzas cost least, so cheese did. Neither the Morgans' (clue 1), the Colliers' (clue 3), the Leonards' (clue 4), nor the Walkers' (clue 6) pizza cost least, so the Nelsons had the $2.00 cheese pizza. The only mathematical possibility in clue 2 is for the mushroom pizza to cost $2.75 and the 16" $2.25. Therefore the 12" pizza was not $2.00 (clue 5), and it cannot have been $3.00 or $3.50 either (also clue 5)—so it cost $2.75, and thus was the mushroom pizza, and the anchovy pizza cost $3.50 (clue 5). The 14" pizza was not one of the two most expensive (clue 4), so it was $2.00—the cheese pizza purchased by the Nelsons; thus the Leonards bought the $2.75 mushroom pizza. Since we now know the 12", 16", and 14" pizzas cost least, the Colliers must have had the $3.50 anchovy pizza, and the $3.00 pizza was the 18" one (clue 3)—leaving the 20" pizza for the Colliers. The 16" pizza wasn't sausage (clue 2)—so the sausage pizza was the 18" one, and the 16" was pepperoni; thus, the Walkers ordered the 18" sausage pizza (clue 6); and the Morgans had the pepperoni. In summary:

Nelsons, cheese, 14", $2.00
Morgans, pepperoni, 16", $2.25
Leonards, mushroom, 12", $2.75
Walkers, sausage, 18", $3.00
Colliers, anchovy, 20", $3.50

18. LETTERS TO THE EDITOR

Mrs. Smith is not Joan (clues 2, 6), so she is Iris; Joan is then the other named female solver, Miss Underwood (clue 7). Vaughn is neither Henry nor Kurt (clue 1), so he is George; he is from a western state (also clue 1), but not from California (clue 5); he lives in Oregon. The Pennsylvanian is not Iris Smith, Kurt, or Joan Underwood (clues 2, 6), and must be Henry. Kurt also lives in an eastern state (clue 1), so he is from New Jersey and is the interior decorator (clue 3); his last name is not Thorpe (also clue 3), so it is Rogers, and Thorpe is Henry's last name. By clues 6 and 7, Kurt Rogers is the cryptogram fan, and Joan Underwood favors mazes. Since George Vaughn lives in Oregon, the crossword fan lives in California (clue 1) and must be Iris Smith; Joan Underwood then lives in Louisiana. George Vaughn is not the quiz fan (clue 5), so he likes diagramless puzzles, and Henry Thorpe favors the quizzes; Vaughn is the teacher (clue 4). Henry Thorpe is neither the artist (clue 2) nor the accountant (clue 5), and must be the engineer. Nor is Californian Iris Smith the accountant (also clue 5); she is the artist, and the accountant is Joan Underwood. In summary, the full names of the solvers, their favorite puzzles, occupations, and residences are:

> Kurt Rogers, cryptograms, interior decorator, New Jersey
> Iris Smith, crosswords, commercial artist, California
> Henry Thorpe, quizzes, engineer, Pennsylvania
> Joan Underwood, mazes, accountant, Louisiana
> George Vaughn, diagramless puzzles, English teacher, Oregon

19. THE MODELS CLUB

Since, from the introduction, only four different heights are involved among the five women, Tracy, who is shorter than three others (clue 1) must be 5'9". Thus, also by clue 1, the oldest of the women is 5'10", and Connie and Mildred are—in one order or the other—5'11" and 6'. Then, by clue 2, Connie is 5'11" and Mildred must be Ms. Keeshan and is 6' tall. Donna and Marie are both 5'10", and Marie is the oldest (clue 2). Neither Mildred Keeshan (clue 2) nor Tracy (clue 4) is one of the two youngest, so Tracy is second oldest, Mildred third (clue 6). Marie's last name begins with "D" (clue 3) but is not Davis (clue 1), so she is Ms. Denny. Donna's last name is Davis (clue 3); she is not the youngest (clue 5), so she is next-to-youngest and Connie is the youngest. Tracy is not Ms. Williams (clue 4), so she is Ms. Hastings, and Connie is Ms. Williams. Thus the five, listed in order from eldest to youngest, are:

> Marie Denny, 5'10"
> Tracy Hastings, 5'9"
> Mildred Keeshan, 6'
> Donna Davis, 5'10"
> Connie Williams, 5'11"

20. PRESIDENTIAL NAMES

Six youngsters are mentioned. They include Brendan, a high school senior (clue 4); two juniors, James Brent and a Bond boy (clue 2); two sophomores, whose middle names are Garfield and Adams (clue 5); and Peter, a freshman (clue 6). Alice, the only girl, must be one of the sophomores; her middle name isn't Adams (clue 1), so it is Garfield. Edward Wilson (clue 3) can only be the junior Bond boy. The second sophomore, by elimination, is John, and his middle name is Adams (clue 5). Edward Wilson Bond isn't related to Alice (clue 3), so her last name is Brent, as is John's (clue 1). James's middle name is Lincoln (clue 7). Brendan's middle name is Monroe, and Peter's is Grant (clue 4). James and John Brent have no other brothers (clue 8) so Brendan and Peter are Bonds. In summary:

> Brendan Monroe Bond, senior
> Edward Wilson Bond, junior
> Peter Grant Bond, freshman
> Alice Garfield Brent, sophomore
> James Lincoln Brent, junior
> John Adams Brent, sophomore

21. ZODIAC FAMILY TREE

Ann is not the oldest daughter (clue 1); neither is Mary nor Olga (clue 2), nor Trudy (clue 4). So the top plaque must be Rosie's. Since Mary's plaque is not one of the two lowest (clue 2), and it cannot be the middle one (clue 6), Mary is the second-oldest daughter. Gemini is thus on the fifth or lowest plaque (clue 6)—along with Leo (clue 4). Capricorn then separates Gemini from Trudy's plaque (clue 3) so is located on the next-to-lowest one; thus Trudy must be the third or middle daughter. Aries, since it is on a plaque higher than Trudy's but is not on Rosie's (clue 4), must be a sign on the next-to-highest plaque, and Sagittarius is on the next-to-lowest one with Capricorn (clue 4). We now know all the signs on the two lowest plaques. Since Libra is on the plaque just above Ann's (clue 1), it must be on the middle plaque and Ann is the fourth-oldest daughter. Olga is thus the youngest, and her plaque the lowest. The other zodiac sign on Trudy's plaque is that of Moon Children (clue 2). Pisces must be on the second plaque (clue 5), with Taurus and Scorpio on the top one. In summary, from top to bottom:

> 1st, Rosie, Taurus & Scorpio
> 2nd, Mary, Aries & Pisces
> 3rd, Trudy, Libra & Moon Children
> 4th, Ann, Capricorn & Sagittarius
> 5th, Olga, Gemini & Leo

22. FAMILY FUN

The names of the Williams children tell us that there are four girls and three boys. The 23-year-old and the 21-year-old are girls (clue 1), as are the 16-year-old and the 13-year-old (clue 4). The boys are therefore 17 (clue 2), 14 (clue 7), and 12 (clue 3). The youngest boy is not Jack (clue 1) or Matt (clue 3), so he is Fred. His hobby is model trains (clue 3), and his girl is Barbara (clue 7). Matt, whose interest is guinea pigs (clue 3), is not 17 (clue 2), so he is 14; his girl is Donna (clue 7). Jack must be the 17-year-old swimmer (clue 2), and his girl is Becky, the only other female mentioned (clue 5) who is not one of the Williams family. Joan's interest is knitting (clue 5). Ruth, who is a high school freshman and goes with Jim (clue 6), cannot be the stamp collector or painter (clue 4), so she is the 13-year-old ballet student (also clue 4). Bill's girl collects stamps (clue 4), and, from the introduction, Russ's girl (fiancée) is either 21 or 23, so she does not paint (clue 4); she must be the one who knits—i.e., Joan. Since Jack is 17, Mary is the 16-year-old (clue 1) who paints (clue 4); her boyfriend must be Bruce. Joan is not 23 (clue 5), so she is 21; the oldest is thus Laura, and she must be Bill's girl, the stamp collector. In summary, from oldest to youngest:

> 23, Laura, stamp collecting, Bill
> 21, Joan, knitting, Russ
> 17, Jack, swimming, Becky
> 16, Mary, painting, Bruce
> 14, Matt, guinea pigs, Donna
> 13, Ruth, ballet, Jim
> 12, Fred, model trains, Barbara

23. METROPOLITAN EXECUTIVES

By clue 1, one of the four works on the first floor, but he is neither Brown nor Block; nor is he Lane (clue 4), so he is Smith. Also by clue 1, one of the men, who is neither Block nor Brown, works on the fourth floor; he must be Lane. By clue 2, one executive is on the fifth floor, by clue 3 it is not Block, so it must be Brown. Block works on either the second or third floor, and the other is empty. By clue 3, he works on the second floor. By clue 2, Brown gets off his bus at the building's southwest corner and uses the south entrance. Lane uses the west entrance (clue 3). By clue 1, Lane must get off his bus at the building's northwest corner, as does Smith; since all the executives use different entrances, Smith uses the north one, since each uses one of the two nearest his stop. Block, by elimination, uses the east entrance. Since the latter's bus stop can be seen from Brown's (clue 1), it is the southeast corner. In summary:

> Block, 2nd floor: east entrance, SE bus stop
> Brown, 5th floor: south entrance, SW bus stop
> Lane, 4th floor: west entrance, NW bus stop
> Smith, 1st floor: north entrance, NW bus stop

24. THE AMBASSADORS

No ambassador was appointed to the country where he can speak the language fluently. Therefore, the ambassador to Italy cannot speak Italian. Nor does he speak Russian or German (clue 2) or Spanish (clue 4). He speaks French. Howard does not speak Italian (clue 5), Russian, German, or French (clue 2), so he is fluent in Spanish. Mr. Kreech is not Peter or Erwin (clue 1), Randy or Howard (clue 4). He is Alan. Since all five men are mentioned in clue 5, one of them must be the French-speaking ambassador to Italy. He is not Alan Kreech or the Spanish-speaking Howard (clue 4), so he is Mr. Carter. The ambassador to Spain is not Alan, Peter, or Erwin (clue 1). Nor is he Howard, since Howard speaks Spanish. Randy will serve in Spain. Randy must be one of the men mentioned in clue 5, so he is the Italian-speaking ambassador. Randy is not Mr. Vance (clue 3) or Mr. Stamey (clue 4); he is Mr. Morley. Howard is not Mr. Stamey (clue 4); he is Mr. Vance. Howard Vance is not ambassador to France (clue 3) or to the U.S.S.R. (clue 5); he will serve in Germany. Alan Kreech is not ambassador to the U.S.S.R. (clue 5); he will serve in France. Mr. Stamey is ambassador to the U.S.S.R. Thus, Mr. Stamey cannot speak Russian; he speaks German. By elimination, Mr. Kreech speaks Russian. Mr. Stamey is not Peter (clue 6); he is Erwin, and Peter is Mr. Carter. In summary:

> Peter Carter, ambassador to Italy, speaks French.
> Alan Kreech, ambassador to France, speaks Russian.
> Randy Morley, ambassador to Spain, speaks Italian.
> Erwin Stamey, ambassador to the U.S.S.R., speaks German.
> Howard Vance, ambassador to Germany, speaks Spanish.

25. THE TEMPS

By clues 1 and 4, Andrea and Ellen were each hired for three or more days. Ms. Thomas was also hired for three or more days and isn't Andrea (clues 1, 6); nor is she Ellen, since Ellen worked two more days than Ms. Young (clue 4) and Ms. Thomas two more days than the one who worked for the stockbrokers (clue 6), and the latter is not Ms. Young (clue 2). If Ms. Thomas worked five days, the one who worked for the stockbrokers for three days (clue 6) would be Andrea (clue 7); Ellen would have worked four days and Ms. Young two (clue 4), contradicting clue 1. Nor did Ellen work five days, since then Ms. Young—who would have to be Andrea—would have worked three (clue 4), and Andrea is not Ms. Young (clue 2). So Andrea is the one who worked five days. Ellen, then, is Ms. Wilson and worked four days, and Ms. Thomas worked three days for the accountants (clue 1). Ms. Young worked two days (clue 4), and the one who worked for the stockbrokers one day (clue 6). The latter is not Ms. Stevens (clue 6); she is Ms. Valley, and Andrea's last name is Stevens. She did not work for the physicians or dentists (clue 9), so she worked for the lawyers. Ellen then worked for the dentists (clue 5), and Ms. Young, by elimination, for the physicians. Since by clue 3 Betsy did not work for the accountants, she is not Ms. Thomas; nor is she Ms. Valley (also clue 3), so she is Ms. Young. Denise isn't Ms. Thomas (clue 8), so Carol is, and Denise is Ms. Valley. In summary:

> Andrea Stevens, lawyers, 5
> Ellen Wilson, dentists, 4
> Carol Thomas, accountants, 3
> Betsy Young, physicians, 2
> Denise Valley, stockbrokers, 1

26. THE TV NEWS PROGRAM

Ross is one of the feature reporters (clue 5), so Archer and Ellis are regulars and are on the air daily, in this order, just before the feature (clue 1). From clue 2, then, Gregg is another feature reporter, the feature comes on as the third topic daily, and Davis and Jones have the fourth and fifth spots regularly. The daily order is thus: Archer, local news; Ellis, sports; feature; Davis, weather; Jones, world news (clue 3). As for the features, Ross appears on Tuesday (clue 1), Gregg Thursday (clue 2), Clark Wednesday, Harris Friday (cluc 4), and Butler, by elimination, Monday. Gardening is the feature either Wednesday or Thursday (clue 5). If the consecutive days for consumerism and food were Monday and Tuesday (clue 6), this would leave no day for the

147

health feature (clue 4). So consumerism is Tuesday's feature and food is Wednesday's. Health is covered Monday (clue 4), gardening Thursday, and child psychology Friday (clue 5). In summary, in order of daily airing:

Local news, Archer
Sports, Ellis
Feature: Mon.: health, Butler
            Tues.: consumerism, Ross
            Wed.: food, Clark
            Thurs.: gardening, Gregg
            Fri.: child psychology, Harris
Weather, Davis
World news, Jones

27. A QUINTUPLE WEDDING

From clues 5 and 6, by pairing the types of bouquets carried by the brides with the boutonnieres worn by the grooms, we know Martha married Mr. Wilder; Betty married Frank Mack; Mr. Black is from Dallas; Mr. Jenson from San Francisco; and Brad and his bride were bound for Rome. By clue 4, Janice is 26 years old, Brad's Rome-bound bride is 24, the sister who married Mr. Jenson from San Francisco is 22, the Hawaii-bound bride is 20, and George's wife is 18. From clue 2, George and his wife planned to honeymoon at the Grand Canyon, and 26-year-old Janice married Ed. Betty is either 20 or 22, but since the 22-year-old married Mr. Jenson, and Betty married Frank Mack, she must be the 20-year-old who by clue 4 honeymooned in Hawaii. By elimination, Steve married the 22-year-old, so he must be Mr. Jenson from San Francisco. Mr. Black from Dallas is not George, since George married the youngest (clue 3), or Brad (clue 6), so he is Ed; Brad's last name is not Wilder (also clue 6), so he is Mr. Alberts, and Mr. Wilder, Martha's husband, is George. Brad Alberts didn't marry Patti (clue 1), so he married Cathy and Patti married Steve Jenson. Also by clue 1, Patti and Steve did not plan a Jamaica honeymoon, so Ed and Janice Black did, and Patti and Steve were bound for Paris. Brad Alberts hailed from neither Boston (clue 1) nor Miami (clue 7), so he must be from New York. Nor is Frank Mack from Boston (clue 1), so he is from Miami, and the Bostonian is George Wilder. In summary:

Brad Alberts from New York married 24-year-old Cathy; they honeymooned in Rome.
Ed Black from Dallas married 26-year-old Janice; they honeymooned in Jamaica.
Steve Jenson from San Francisco married 22-year-old Patti; they honeymooned in Paris.
Frank Mack from Miami married 20-year-old Betty; they honeymooned in Hawaii.
George Wilder from Boston married 18-year-old Martha; they honeymooned at the Grand Canyon.

28. COSMETICS COSTS

Helen bought Terrific Odor perfume (clue 1). Neither she (clue 1), Sue (clue 6), Betty, nor Jackie (clue 7) is Ms. Smith; it's Ann's surname, and she bought Pink Icing lipstick (also clue 7). Neither Sue nor Jackie was the woman who bought Perfect Scent perfume and Red Moon lipstick (clue 5), so Betty did. Ms. Hall is neither Sue, Jackie (clue 4), nor Helen (clue 6); she is Betty. Ms. Brown isn't Helen (clue 1) or Jackie (clue 3), so she is Sue. Jackie isn't Ms. Jones (clue 6), so her surname is Abbott, and Helen is then Ms. Jones. By clue 3, Helen Jones bought Melon Mellow lipstick. She spent $10 more than Ann Smith (clue 8); by clue 1, then, she spent $20 and Ann $10, and Sue Brown spent $16. Betty Hall spent $8 and Jackie Abbott $24 (clue 4). By clue 2, Sue bought Great Smell perfume, Jackie Tangerine Talks lipstick, and Ann Ideal Essence perfume. By elimination, Sue bought Coral Kiss lipstick and Jackie Divine Fragrance perfume. In summary, from least to most spent:

Betty Hall: Perfect Scent, Red Moon, $8
Ann Smith: Ideal Essence, Pink Icing, $10
Sue Brown: Great Smell, Coral Kiss, $16
Helen Jones: Terrific Odor, Melon Mellow, $20
Jackie Abbott: Divine Fragrance, Tangerine Talks, $24

29. MOTHER–DAUGHTER BANQUET

Mrs. Lee (clue 1), Mrs. Mix, and Mrs. Jones (clue 5) are all grandmothers; therefore the two who are not are Mrs. Nye and Mrs. Koon, and the latter sat at table 1 (clue 1). The daughters of Mrs. Nye and Mrs. Koon are, in one order or the other, the professor and Mrs. Dill (clue 2); the professor is not Mrs. Nye's daughter (clue 4), so the professor sat with her mother, Mrs. Koon, at table 1, and Mrs. Nye's daughter is Mrs. Dill. The professor is not Mrs. Cox (clue 1), Mrs. Able, or Mrs. Eton (clue 6); she is Mrs. Best. The attorney is not Mrs. Cox (clue 1), Mrs. Dill (clues 1,2), or Mrs. Eton (clue 7), so she is Mrs. Able; her mother is not Mrs. Lee (clue 1) or Mrs. Mix (clue 5), so she is Mrs. Jones. Mrs. Cox is not Mrs. Lee's daughter (clue 1); she is Mrs. Mix's, and Mrs. Lee's daughter is Mrs. Eton. Mrs. Cox is neither the engineer (clue 3) nor the pharmacist (clue 5), so she is the accountant. Since a grandmother had to sit at table 3 (clue 8), Mrs. Nye and her daughter did not sit there, nor did they sit at table 2 or table 5 (clue 4); they were at table 4. Mrs. Jones and her daughter, the attorney, did not sit at table 5 (clue 7) or table 3 (clue 8); they were at table 2. Mrs. Eton was not at table 5 (clue 7); so she and her mother were at table 3; therefore she is not the engineer (clue 3), she is Mrs. Eton, the pharmacist. By elimination, Mrs. Dill is the engineer, and Mrs. Cox and her mother sat at table 5. In summary, the five mothers and daughters, and the tables at which they sat are:

> Mrs. Jones and Mrs. Able, the attorney—table 2
> Mrs. Koon and Mrs. Best, the professor—table 1
> Mrs. Lee and Mrs. Eton, the pharmacist—table 3
> Mrs. Mix and Mrs. Cox, the accountant—table 5
> Mrs. Nye and Mrs. Dill, the engineer—table 4

30. CONDO COMPLEX

The Newells live on the tennis-court side (clue 5), as do the Riders (clue 9) and the Parkers (clue 12). Agatha, who lives between the Parkers and the Riders (clue 2), then must be Mrs. Newell and live in #2. Laura is then in #3 (clue 5). By clue 8, Kate must also be on the tennis-court side, so she must live in #1. Her last name is not Rider (also clue 8), so it is Parker, and Laura is Mrs. Rider. Harriet lives in either #5 or #6 (clue 6), as does Carol (clue 7), so, by elimination, Frances is the woman in #4. Edward lives on the tennis-court side (clue 4), as do Ira (clue 1) and Bruce (clue 3). Kate Parker's husband is neither Bruce (clue 8) nor Edward (clue 11), so he is Ira. Bruce is not Agatha Newell's husband (clue 3), so Edward is, and Bruce is Mr. Rider. Since Frances lives in #4, by clue 10 Donald lives in #5 and the O'Brians in #6. By clue 6, then, Mrs. Minton is Frances, Harriet is Donald's wife, and Carol must be Mrs. O'Brian. And since Jeffrey isn't Mr. Minton (also clue 6), he must be Mr. O'Brian. By elimination, Mr. Minton is George, and Donald and Harriet are the Quades. In summary:

> #1: Kate & Ira Parker
> #2: Agatha & Edward Newell
> #3: Laura & Bruce Rider
> #4: Frances & George Minton
> #5: Harriet & Donald Quade
> #6: Carol & Jeffrey O'Brian

31. THE CAR POOL

The Mayor's first stop is not for the Police Chief (clue 2), Fire Chief (clue 3), Buildings Inspector (clue 4), or City Engineer (clue 5); it is for the Parks Director. The last stop is not for the Police Chief (clue 2), Fire Chief (clue 3), or Buildings Inspector (clue 4); it is for the City Engineer. Thus, the fourth stop is for Steve and the third is for Mr. Ashton (clue 5); since there are at least 3 pickups before Frank, and Steve is fourth, Frank must be last and is the City Engineer (clue 1). Ashton, the third stop, is not Walter or Keith (clue 5); he is David. Thus, since David Ashton is the Mayor's third pickup, the Police Chief is neither second nor fourth (clue 2), and must be Ashton. Steve is then Mr. Trent, and Keith is picked up second (also clue 2), leaving Walter to be the Parks Director who is picked up first. The Building Inspector must be fourth (clue 4), so he is Steve Trent, and Frank Eller is fifth (also clue 4). By elimination, Keith must be the Fire Chief.

The Fire Chief is not Mr. Morris (clue 3) so he is Mr. Dewey, and Mr. Morris is Walter, the Parks Director (clue 3). In summary, the mayor picks up the five in the following order:

Parks Director Walter Morris
Fire Chief Keith Dewey
Police Chief David Ashton
Buildings Inspector Steve Trent
City Engineer Frank Eller

32. PLAYING THE STOCK MARKET

Since 25 points separated the closing prices of the third-highest and lowest-priced stocks (clue 4), and 5 points separated Black Gold from the lowest-priced stock (clue 3), Black Gold sold for the fourth-highest price. If Zeroz were the highest-priced stock, by clue 1 it would be worth only 20, which is two times the 10-point difference between its price and that of Polk; but since clue 4 tells us that there was a 25-point difference between two of the stocks, the highest-priced stock must have closed above 20 points and could not be Zeroz. Since neither Polk (clue 1) nor Siding Aluminum (clue 2) sold highest, Nadir Markets stock did. By clue 1, Polk sold at less than Zeroz and at half the price of Nadir; Siding sold at one-quarter of Nadir's price (clue 2). Zeroz, Polk, and Siding then closed second-highest, third highest, and lowest, in that order. Since Nadir's closing price was four times that of Siding (clue 2) and two times that of Polk (clue 1), then Polk's closing price must have been two times that of Siding. By clue 4 we know that Polk closed 25 points higher than Siding, so Polk's closing prices must have been two times 25—or 50—while Siding closed at 25 points. Then Nadir's price was 100, Zeroz's 60 (clue 1), and Black Gold's was 30 (clue 3). Neither Zeroz (clue 1), Siding (clue 2), Black Gold (clue 3), nor Nadir (clue 5) stock increased the most, so Polk Motors did. Since the lowest increase was 2 points (clue 3), Zeroz stock did not increase least (clue 1); nor did Nadir Markets (clue 2), or Black Gold (clue 5). Siding Aluminum then increased least, by 2 points. Nadir was up then 4 (clue 2); Black Gold up 5 (clue 5); Polk up 10 (clue 3), and Zeroz up 8 (clue 1). In summary:

Nadir Markets, up 4 to 100
Zeroz Corp., up 8 to 60
Polk Motors, up 10 to 50
Black Gold Petroleum, up 5 to 30
Siding Aluminum, up 2 to 25

33. FRIENDS AND ACTIVITIES

Jane plays golf (clue 7). She is not Ms. Nye or Ms. King (clue 3), and she is not Ms. Lane (clue 4) or Ms. Munn (clue 5), so she is Ms. Orr. Her second interest is cycling, and that is one of Holly's interests as well (clue 1). Ms. Munn, who doesn't cycle (clue 5), is a third woman, and she and Ellie, a fourth woman, are both baseball fans (clue 2). Ms. Munn isn't Fran (also clue 2), so she is Gail. Ellie is not Ms. Lane (clue 4), nor, since she is a baseball fan, can she be Ms. King (clue 6), so her last name is Nye. Ellie Nye and Gail Munn, the other baseball fan (clue 2), in one order or the other, have canoeing and moviegoing as their second activity (clues 6, 7). Ellie Nye cannot be the canoer, however, because clue 4 states that she also shares an activity with Ms. Lane; since we know she goes to basketball games with Gail Munn, going canoeing with Ms. King would give her three activities instead of two. Therefore, Gail Munn goes canoeing with Ms. King and Ellie Nye shares moviegoing with Ms. Lane. By clue 4, Ms. Lane also plays golf with Jan Orr. By elimination, Holly's last name is King, she goes cycling and canoeing, and Ms. Lane is Fran. In summary:

Holly King, cycling and canoeing
Fran Lane, movies and golf
Gail Munn, baseball and canoeing
Ellie Nye, baseball and movies
Jane Orr, golf and cycling

34. A RACE TO THE FINISH

By clues 1 and 2, Johnson rode Lucky and was first, Smith was second, Karen was third, Doyle was fourth, Kane was fifth, Hopeful was ninth, and Brown was tenth. From clue 3, Hanson had to be among the first five and so must be Karen, while Sue placed eighth. The three horses described in clue 4 cannot have placed first, third, and fifth, since Kane placed fifth; or third, fifth, and seventh, since Karen placed third; or fourth, sixth, and eighth, since Sue placed eighth; or sixth, eighth, and tenth, since Brown placed tenth. If they placed fifth, seventh, and ninth, that would mean Mr. Farrell (mentioned in clue 8) and Cathy Cash (mentioned in the introduction) were sixth and seventh (in one order or the other), Sue's surname would be Potts (by elimination), and she would place just behind Jubilee. But that contradicts clue 6; so the horses described in clue 4 must have placed second, fourth, and sixth—i.e., Henry is Smith, Doyle rode Jubilee, and Bates finished sixth. Cathy Cash finished seventh or ninth, as did Mr. Farrell, so Sue's last name is Potts. By clue 6, then Bates rode Delaware and Kitty Kat, ridden by Ed, was in seventh place. Ed must be Mr. Farrell, while Cathy Cash rode Hopeful. By clue 7, the only possibility is that Jack was first, Best Boy was second, and Chuck finished in fourth place. By clue 5 Pete must have finished fifth and John tenth. John Brown rode Penny Money, while Pete rode Katie Bell (clue 2). Delaware's rider, by elimination, was Adam. Prideful finished in eighth place (clue 8). Karen Hanson, by elimination, rode Foxy Lady. In summary:

#1, Jack Johnson, Lucky
#2, Henry Smith, Best Boy
#3, Karen Hanson, Foxy Lady
#4, Chuck Doyle, Jubilee
#5, Pete Kane, Katie Bell
#6, Adam Bates, Delaware
#7, Ed Farrell, Kitty Kat
#8, Sue Potts, Prideful
#9, Cathy Cash, Hopeful
#10, John Brown, Penny Money

35. CONSUMER COUPONS

The cereal coupon, for a rebate, expired October 31 (clue 4). The $2 rebate offer and Clark's offer expired, in one order or the other, on March 15 and May 1 (clue 3). Strong's offer was not the $2 rebate or one of the offers expiring on January 31 or December 31 (clue 1), so it was the rebate on cereal. Abbot's free-product offer (clue 7) did not expire on January 31 (clue 2), so it expired December 31. The cosmetics rebate offer was not Abbot's or the first to expire (clue 2) and was not Clark's (clue 6), so the $2 rebate was for cosmetics. From clue 5, if the B&D coupon expired January 31, then the cosmetics rebate would be $1.50 conflicting with what we have established. If B&D's expired May 1, that would mean the coupon expiring December 31 offered a $1.50 rebate when in fact we know it offered a free product. Therefore, the only possibility is that the B&D $2 cosmetics rebate offer expired March 15, the Clark bread coupon expired May 1, and Strong's cereal rebate was for $1.50. Folk's must have been the coupon expiring January 31; it was not for paper towels (clue 6), so it was for soap, and Abbot's was for paper towels. Folk's rebate was $1 (clue 2). Clark's, by elimination, was 75¢. In summary:

Folk soap, $1 rebate, January 31
B&D cosmetics, $2 rebate, March 15
Clark bread, 75¢ rebate, May 1
Strong cereal, $1.50 rebate, October 31
Abbot paper towels, free product, December 31

36. THE VOYAGES

By clue 1, the cheapest ship made the shortest voyage, 15 days; it was not to the north (clue 2), east (clue 3), or south (clue 5), so it was to the west. Its captain wasn't Zippo (clue 2) or Harko (clue 3). If its captain was Gaucho, its cost would have been 12,000 simoleons (clue 4), that of the ship which made the longest voyage 14,000 (clue 1), and a third ship over 14,000 (clue 9)—a total of over 40,000; since Queen Lulu's total expense was 42,000, that would leave less than 2000 for the fourth ship. So the captain of the cheapest ship was Chito. His ship was not the *Monkey Business* (clue 6), *Duck Soup,* or *Horse Feathers* (clue 7); it was the *Animal Crackers,* and it cost 6000 simoleons (clue 5). Therefore, the longest voyage, 40 days, was made to Banana Island in a ship that cost 8000 simoleons (clues 1, 9). Gaucho's ship cost 12,000 simoleons (clue 4). Since the total spent was 42,000, the remaining ship cost 16,000. By clue 7, Gaucho captained the *Duck Soup,* and the 16,000-simoleon ship was the *Horse Feathers;* the 8000-simoleon ship, by elimination, was the *Monkey Business.* The *Animal Crackers* went to neither Pineapple Island (clue 8) nor Orange Island (clue 9), so it went to Coconut Island. By clue 8, then, another ship—either the *Horse Feathers* or the *Duck Soup*—had a 30-day voyage to Pineapple Island. If it was *Horse Feathers,* then—since *Animal Crackers* sailed west—by clue 2, its captain would have been not Zippo but Harko, and Zippo would then be the captain on the *Monkey Business,* which made the 40-day voyage, with the fourth ship making a 20-day voyage. That ship would have to be *Duck Soup*—which clue 2 says it was not. So it was Gaucho's *Duck Soup* that made the 30-day trip to Pineapple Island; the *Horse Feathers,* by elimination, went to Orange Island. By clue 2, the northern voyage can only have been that of *Horse Feathers* and must have taken 20 days, while Zippo captained the *Monkey Business*—and Harko the *Horse Feathers.* The *Duck Soup* sailed south (clue 5), Zippo's ship east. In summary:

> Chito's *Animal Crackers:* 6000, west to Coconut I., 15 days
> Gaucho's *Duck Soup:* 12,000 south to Pineapple I., 30 days
> Harko's *Horse Feathers:* 16,000, north to Orange I., 20 days
> Zippo's *Monkey Business:* 8000, east to Banana I., 40 days

37. MINIATURE GOLF

For a total of six or less, which Bob made (clue 2), it would be necessary to have at least two holes-in-one; he therefore played the blue ball and made holes-in-one on the first and fourth holes (clue 1). Since they were the *only* holes-in-one, he shot two on each of the other holes and was the winner with a total of six. Dan did not play the red (clue 3) or yellow ball (clue 5); his ball was green. Alan scored a six on the fourth hole (clue 6), so his score was at least twelve. The player of the red ball, whose total score was ten (clue 3), was then Carl, and Alan's ball was the yellow one. Dan went over par just once, with a four on the second hole (clue 5). Carl was over par on two holes (clue 3), so the player who scored two on each of the first three holes (clue 4) was Alan, whose total was thus twelve. The three scores established thus far, in ranking order, were six, ten, and twelve, so Dan, who placed third (clue 5), scored a total of eleven, and must have hit exactly par on the first, third, and fourth holes. The only possibility for Carl, since he was over par on two holes, is that he was one over on the first and fourth holes and one under on the second and third. In summary, in winning order, with the scores on the four holes in order:

> Bob, blue: 1, 2, 2, 1 = 6
> Carl, red: 3, 2, 2, 3, = 10
> Dan, green: 2, 4, 3, 2 = 11
> Alan, yellow: 2, 2, 2, 6 = 12

38. ANNIVERSARY PARTY

Since the Greens included two brothers and two sisters, and the wives took their husbands' surnames, there are two couples named Green (the two brothers and their wives), one named Smith (a Green sister and her husband), and one named Stout (the other Green sister and her husband). The women who married the Green brothers each have three brothers-in-law (counting the Green sisters' husbands), so by clue 5, Jean is one of the Green sisters (Mrs. Smith or Mrs. Stout), and her only brother-in-law must be the husband of her sister Jane. Joan and Nancy are then the two married to the Green brothers. By clue 2, then, Joan and Nancy must be sisters, while Harry married one of the Green sisters and is either Mr. Smith or Mr. Stout. He is Mr. Smith, and his wife is Jane (clue 3), so Jean's last name is Stout. The anniversary couple weren't the Stouts (clue 1), Nancy and her husband (clue 4), or Jane and Harry Smith (clue 5), so they were Joan and her husband. Nancy's husband isn't George (clue 2) or Paul (clue 4), so he is Bill. Joan's husband isn't Paul, who brought a gift (clue 4), so he is George, and Paul is Mr. Stout.

The Stouts brought either champagne or fruit (clue 4), but not champagne (clue 1), so they brought fruit; Nancy and Bill Green then brought champagne (clue 4) and the Smiths, by elimination, brought the theater tickets. In summary:

> George & Joan Green, anniversary couple
> Bill & Nancy Green, champagne
> Paul & Jean Stout, fruit basket
> Harry & Jane Smith, theater tickets

39. THE HOME-RUN CHAMPS

The man with the highest batting average was not Banks (clue 1) or Rodgers (clue 2). By clue 1, Banks's average was no higher than 306—so South's can have been no higher than 312 (clue 3). The ranks for batting averages and for home runs were in reverse order. Since Warner's batting average was higher than Banks's (clue 1), Warner had fewer home runs than Banks; thus, by clue 3, Jensen had more homers than Banks—hence a lower batting average. Warner is the only one who could have had the highest batting average, 316; he therefore had the least number of home runs, 32. By clue 1, Banks's batting average was 306. Both Rodgers and Jensen had more home runs than Banks (clue 2), so Banks must have had either 34 or 36. If Banks had 34, then, by clue 3, Jensen would have had 36—but that is impossible, since another man ranked between them (clue 2). Banks must have had 36 homers and, by clue 2, Rodgers had 38, and Jensen 40; South, by elimination, had 34. Since Jensen had the highest number of home runs, he had the lowest batting average, 300. Rodgers had more homers than Banks, hence a lower batting average, i.e., either 302 or 304. If Rodgers's average were 302, then, by clue 3, South's would be 310, contradicting clue 2. Rodgers's average must have been 304, making South's 308. In summary, you should have:

	home runs	batting average
Jensen	40	300
Rodgers	38	304
Banks	36	306
South	34	308
Warner	32	316

40. NEWSPAPER FEATURES

There are precisely two special features appearing each day (clue 3). On Tuesday, *The Eagle* publishes both food news and its second special topic, since no other paper runs a feature that day (clue 1). *The Clarion*'s special-feature days are Monday, Thursday, and Saturday, and since neither of the other papers has a feature on Thursday (clue 4), both its special departments appear that day. Since business news appears three times a week (clue 2), but not on Saturday (clue 3), that is not one of *The Clarion*'s topics, nor is travel (clue 2). It must feature either music or theater on Saturday—with the other featured by a different paper (clue 3)—and its second special topic must be society news. Its Saturday feature is thus music (clue 5), it runs both features on Thursday, and, since both subjects are featured twice a week (clue 2), it features society news on Monday. If *The Eagle*'s second special topic were business—i.e., if it ran both food and business news on Tuesday—then, since food is featured twice a week and business three times (clue 2), there would be a second day on which both food and business were featured, contradicting clue 3. *The Bugle*, therefore, runs business news Monday, Wednesday, and Friday, and it is *The Eagle* that runs the theater feature on Saturday (and also on Tuesday). The Wednesday-only travel feature (clue 2) must appear in *The Bugle*. The second feature appearing on Friday must be *The Eagle*'s news of food. In summary:

	Mon.	Tues.	Wed.	Thurs.	Fri.	Sat.
The Bugle	business	—	business, travel	—	business	—
The Clarion	society	—	—	music, society	—	music
The Eagle	—	food, theater	—	—	food	theater

41. CIRCUS TIME

From clues 4 and 5, the order of performances is as follows: first, Claudia's husband and Sharon; second, Marty and Mrs. Smith; third, Mr. Smith ("Juda Jewel"); fourth, John, alias "Flash"; last, the lion tamer and Claudia. Sharon's partner (Claudia's husband) is Harry (clue 2). Also by clue 2, the Beaches are Marty and Marsha, and Christine's last name is Miller, so the Smiths must be Fred and Nancy. By elimination, Dan must be the last performer. The next-to-last female performer is not Christine Miller (clue 1), so she is Marsha Beach, and Christine is Fred Smith's partner. The latter's husband is neither John ("Flash") (clue 1) nor Harry (clue 2), so "Skip" is Dan. Harry and Claudia aren't the Hogans (clue 2), so they are the Herons; John and Sharon must be the Hogans. Harry isn't "Dancy Dart" (clue 3), so he is "Pompy," and "Dancy Dart" is Marty Beach. Since Sharon Hogan is Harry Heron's partner, he must be the trapeze artist (clue 2). John ("Flash") is neither the elephant trainer nor the clown (clue 7) so he is the bareback rider. Nor is Nancy's husband, Fred, the elephant trainer (clue 6); he must be the clown, and Marty Beach is the elephant trainer. In summary, the acts in order of performance are:

> Harry ("Pompy") Heron, trapeze artist, and Sharon Hogan
> Marty ("Dancy Dart") Beach, elephant trainer, and Nancy Smith
> Fred ("Juda Jewel") Smith, clown, and Christine Miller
> John ("Flash") Hogan, bareback rider, and Marsha Beach
> Dan ("Skip") Miller, lion tamer, and Claudia Heron

42. FLYING FROM NEW YORK TO FLORIDA

The number of flights from LaGuardia to Fort Lauderdale was the average of the numbers of flights from the three airports to Fort Lauderdale (clue 6); therefore, one-third of the Fort Lauderdale flights were from LaGuardia. Since the total number of flights to each destination was the same (clue 4), one-third of the Miami flights were from Newark (clue 8); one-half of them were from LaGuardia (clue 2), leaving one-sixth of them from JFK. The smallest number of flights, the four on Benson's route (clue 1), were either from JFK to Miami or from Newark to Fort Lauderdale (clue 6). If there had been four from Newark to Fort Lauderale, by clue 6 there would have been six from LaGuardia and eight from JFK, or eighteen Fort Lauderdale flights in all, and, as already noted, the same number to Miami. The one-sixth of the Miami flights that left from JFK would then be only three, contradicting clue 1. Therefore, Benson's route was from JFK to Miami, which had four flights, and there were twenty-four flights to each destination. Then, by clue 2, the other flights to Miami were twelve from LaGuardia and eight from Newark. To Fort Lauderdale, there were eight from LaGuardia (clue 8), ten from JFK, and six from Newark (clue 6). Allen's route was Newark to Fort Lauderdale, Fox's LaGuardia to Miami (clue 5). By clue 7, since we know the numbers of flights on Allen's routes (six) and Benson's routes (four), we find that Dawson must have flown the route with ten flights—JFK to Fort Lauderdale— and Ewig one of the routes with eight flights (clue 7). Since Ewig did not leave from Fox's airport, LaGuardia (clue 3), he flew from Newark to Miami, and by elimination, Carlson flew from LaGuardia to Fort Lauderdale. The routes (with the number of flights on the route) are:

> Allen: Newark to Fort Lauderdale (6)
> Benson: JFK to Miami (4)
> Carlson: LaGuardia to Fort Lauderdale (8)
> Dawson: JFK to Fort Lauderdale (10)
> Ewig: Newark to Miami (8)
> Fox: LaGuardia to Miami (12)

43. SEMINARY GRADUATES

The future seminary professor did not rank first or second (clue 4) or fifth (clue 1). Nor was he fourth, for since all five are mentioned in clue 4, that would make Pete second and then there would be no way for Carter to have ranked exactly three places higher than Ted, as clue 4 also asserts. The future seminary professor must therefore be third. So by clue 4, Pete is first, Carter second, Ted fifth, and the church pastor, the only remaining position, fourth. Pete was single throughout his seminary years (clue 2), and the student who is now the university chaplain got married in his second year of school (clue 5), so they are not the same person. Nor is Ted the chaplain (clue 3), so the chaplain is Carter. Pete and Ted must be the overseas missionary and marriage counselor, though not necessarily respectively. Consequently, Roy, who by clue 5 is not the chaplain or the future seminary professor, is the church pastor. Since Evans is not Roy (clue 5), Evans is not the church pastor; he is also not the future seminary professor (also clue 5), or the overseas missionary (clue 6), so he's the marriage counselor. By clues 2 and 5, Pete is not Evans; Pete, then is the overseas missionary, and Evans's first name is Ted. Pete's last name is not Jacobsen (clue 2) or Brentley (clue 6), so it is Anderson. By clues 2 and 5, Roy is not Jacobsen, so his last name is Brentley. Jeff is not Jacobsen (clue 2) so he's Carter and, by elimination, Eric is Jacobsen; also by elimination, he is the future seminary professor. In summary:

> Pete Anderson, first, overseas missionary
> Jeff Carter, second, university chaplain
> Eric Jacobsen, third, future seminary professor
> Roy Brentley, fourth, church pastor
> Ted Evans, fifth, marriage counselor

44.   PRACTICE MAKES PERFECT

Clue 4 lists all six girls: the tennis player, who has been taking lessons for five months; two—Sue and the skater—who have been taking lessons for less time; and three—Ginger and the swimmer and the one who has taken lessons for twenty months, who have been at their activities longer. By clue 5, the dancer has taken lessons longer than at least two of the others, and the number of months she has been studying is divisible by two and also by three, so she can only be Ginger. By clue 1, then, her last name is Sweet, and Jenny takes piano lessons; the latter can only be the girl who has been taking lessons for twenty months. Sue, by elimination, is taking golf lessons, so her surname is Baker (clue 3), Cathy Brown, who cannot have taken lessons for five or fewer months (clue 3), must be the swimmer. By clue 5, dancer Ginger Sweet (who has taken lessons for more than five months) has taken lessons three times as long as Sue Baker (who has taken lessons for fewer than five months) and also twice as long as another girl. There are just two possibilities: Ginger has taken lessons for six months and Sue for two, or Ginger has taken lessons for twelve months and Sue for four. By clue 3, Ginger has taken lessons four months longer than Sue. So by clues 3 and 5, Ginger has taken lessons for six months, Sue for two, and Cathy for twelve. The Johnson girl, who has taken lessons for only three months (clue 5), must be the skater. By clue 2, the Jensen girl is the tennis player and her first name is Barb, while Laurie is the Johnson girl. Jenny's last name by elimination, is Smith. In summary:

> Sue Baker: golf, 2 months.
> Cathy Brown: swimming, 12 months
> Barb Jensen: tennis, 5 months
> Laurie Johnson: skating, 3 months
> Jenny Smith: piano, 20 months
> Ginger Sweet: dancing, 6 months

45.   THE FAMILY PETS

Mr. and Mrs. Day are the same age (clue 1). Two of the children are twins (clue 3); they are a boy and a girl, and they have an older brother (clues 3, 9), who cares for the hamster, Jiggs (clues 3, 7). Lee, who takes care of Flip, is Mr. or Mrs. Day (clue 6). Three of the Days are males, so they are the three of the same sex mentioned in clue 2; Pat is the older son. If Mr. Day took care of Tip and the boy twin the dog, Mrs. Day would be Lee, the girl twin could care for the rabbit (clue 4), and the dog's name would be Dibs (clues 5, 8). Mr. Day would then care for the cat and Mrs. Day would be Sal (clue 5)—contradicting the earlier inference that she would be Lee. Therefore, the boy twin takes care of Tip and Mr. Day the dog. Chris is Mrs. Day (clue 2), and Mr. Day is Lee. The one who cares for Dibs must be female, so from clue 5, she is Mrs. Day, the girl twin cares for the cat, and the boy twin is Sal. Tip is the rabbit (clue 8). By elimination, Dibs is a bird, the girl twin is Val, and the cat's name is Gog. In summary:

Mr. Lee Day: dog Flip
Mrs. Chris Day: bird Dibs
older son, Pat: hamster Jiggs
boy twin, Sal: rabbit Tip
girl twin, Val: cat Gog

46.   THE MARTIAL ARTS

By clue 4, Hale's class is either Monday or Tuesday. If it were Tuesday, Waldo's class would be Wednesday and Power's Friday, leaving the boxer and Edwin three days apart instead of two, contradicting clue 4. So Hale's class is Monday, Waldo's Tuesday, Power's Thursday, Edwin's Friday, and the boxer's Wednesday. By clue 3 we know that Strong teaches either Wednesday or Thursday, and since Power's day is Thursday, Strong must be the boxing teacher on Wednesday, and Monday, Hale, the librarian's. Stout and the druggist, in one order or the other, are the Tuesday and Wednesday instructors (clue 2); but Strong coaches on Wednesday, so Stout must be Waldo, the Tuesday coach—thus, the druggist is boxer Strong, the printer is Power, and the kung fu instructor is Edwin—who must be the jeweler (clue 3), and, by elimination, his last name is Hardy. Waldo Stout then is the accountant—and since neither he nor Monday coach Hale is the wrestler (clue 1), the wrestling class must be held on Thursday and Power is the teacher. Waldo isn't the karate instructor (clue 6), so he teaches judo, and librarian Hale is the karate instructor. Homer teaches earlier in the week than Strong (clue 5), so he is the Monday coach; since Strong isn't Albert (also clue 5), he's Clarence, and Albert is Power. In summary:

> Monday—karate, by Homer Hale, librarian
> Tuesday—judo, by Waldo Stout, accountant
> Wednesday—boxing, by Clarence Strong, druggist
> Thursday—wrestling, by Albert Power, printer
> Friday—kung fu, by Edwin Hardy, jeweler

47.   ONCE-A-WEEK TREAT

Since two of the five treats were the same price (clue 3), there were no more than four different prices. By clue 6, then, the four prices were represented, in descending order, by the most expensive treat, Ms. Hacket's purchase, the doughnut bought at Tasty Treat, and the cherry-filled bismarck; the doughnut cost 5¢ more than the bismarck, Ms. Hacket's treat 15¢ more than the doughnut. The treat that cost the most was not the Danish (clue 3) or the cinnamon twist (clue 4), so it was the crescent roll. The purchase at Yummy Yum was not the Danish (clue 1), the cinnamon twist, or the crescent (clue 4), so it was the bismarck. By clue 3, the two bought at the same price did not include the crescent roll; and since these two were the treat bought at Goody Good and the Danish, they can only be the two bought at the second-highest price; i.e., Ms. Hacket purchased one of them. The Danish was bought by Paula (clue 1), who is not Ms. Hacket (clue 7)—so the two treats were Paula's Danish and Ms. Hacket's cinnamon twist, the latter purchased at Goody Good (clue 3). By clue 8, Paula bought her treat at Baker's Best and Ms. Hart bought the crescent roll; the latter, by elimination, was purchased at Dandy Dough. Jane is Ms. Hacket and Sandy is Ms. Hart (clue 9). Dot bought the doughnut and Ms. Wilson the bismarck (clue 5); the latter, by elimination, is Helen. Paula is not Ms. Forest (clue 2); she is Ms. Adams, and Ms. Forest is Dot. We know by clue 6 the price of Jane's and Paula's treats was 20¢ more than that of the bismarck bought at Yummy Yum; by clue 4, it was also twice that price and 10¢ less than the crescent roll. Jane and Paula, then, each paid 40¢, the bismarck was 20¢, the doughnut 25¢, and the crescent roll 50¢. In summary:

> Sandy Hart: 50¢ for crescent roll, Dandy Dough
> Paula Adams: 40¢ for Danish, Baker's Best
> Jane Hacket: 40¢ for cinnamon twist, Goody Good
> Dot Forest: 25¢ for doughnut, Tasty Treat
> Helen Wilson: 20¢ for bismarck, Yummy Yum

Each team played each other once, thus five games in all per team. Since, from the introduction, the six teams all had different win–loss records, the only possible way this could happen would be if each team defeated all those who finished behind it and lost to all those who finished ahead of it. Thus, the 1st-place team had a 5–0 record, the 2nd-place team had a 4–1 record, the 3rd-place team finished 3–2, the 4th-place one had a 2–3 record, the 5th-place team finished 1–4, and the 6th-place team was winless at 0–5. By clue 1, the Robins finished in 1st place and West was the 2nd-place team. They were not the Hawks (clue 7). From clue 3, then, the Hawks placed 3rd or 4th, Suburban placed 4th or 5th, and Osgood's team finished 5th or 6th. From clue 2, the Cardinals also placed either 3rd or 4th. Also by clue 2, the Falcons therefore placed 2nd, so they are the West team. Kilmer's team, defeated by the Cardinals (clue 2), is not the Hawks (clue 5), and thus, like Osgood's team, placed either 5th or 6th. South placed no higher than 4th and is not coached by Kilmer (clue 2) or Osgood (clue 8), so by clue 2 the Cardinals placed 3rd and the South team, who must be the Hawks, placed 4th. James isn't South's coach (clue 8), and we've already determined that the teams coached by Kilmer and Osgood are, in one order or the other, 5th and 6th. So, by clue 6, James is West's coach, and North's team placed 1st and must be the Robins. Since Miller's team was defeated by Central (clue 4), it must be the 4th-place South Hawks, and the Central team is the Cardinals. Suburban placed 5th, Osgood's school 6th (clue 3), and Suburban's coach must be Kilmer. East, by elimination, is Osgood's school. It's not the Eagles (clue 9), so it's the Orioles, and Suburban is the Eagles. Lewis is not the coach of the North Robins (clue 1), so Nichols is, and Lewis coaches the Central Cardinals. In summary:

> 1st—North Robins, Nichols (5–0)
> 2nd—West Falcons, James (4–1)
> 3rd—Central Cardinals, Lewis (3–2)
> 4th—South Hawks, Miller (2–3)
> 5th—Suburban Eagles, Kilmer (1–4)
> 6th—East Orioles, Osgood (0–5)

49. JOHN'S GUESSES

Since, by clue 1, there was a different number in each of the three categories, these can only have been one, two, and three. There were exactly two blue-collar workers (clue 2) and more than one white-collar worker (clue 3); there must have been three of the latter and one professional. John's guesses totaled the same (clue 1). The two blue-collar workers were Sue and Ryder (clue 2), and the one professional was Lee (clue 5). Two of the three white-collar workers, about whom John guessed wrong, were Pat and Olsen (clue 4). Since he assigned the white-collar workers to all of the three different categories (clue 3), he must have thought Pat and Olsen, in one order or the other, blue-collar and professional—and since he guessed there was only one professional in the group, that one was Pat King (clue 6), and he thought Olsen was a blue-collar worker. He was then wrong about Lee, the actual professional—whose last name is not Butler (clue 1) or Tonks (clue 5) and must be Faber. Ms. Butler, about whom John guessed right (clue 1), was either Sue or the third white-collar worker. If the latter, then Chris, also the subject of a correct guess (clue 1), would be Ryder; Dale, wrongly identified, would be Olsen, and Ms. Butler's first name would be Edward. Therefore Ms. Butler is Sue, while Chris is the third white-collar worker. Since John wrongly guessed that Dale was a blue-collar worker (clue 6), Dale is Olsen. Since Chris is a white-collar worker, Ryder's first name is Edward, and, by elimination, Chris's surname is Tonks. John guessed both Edward Ryder and Lee Faber were white-collar workers. In summary, with John's guesses in parentheses:

> blue-collar: Sue Butler (blue-collar), Edward Ryder (white-collar)
> white-collar: Pat King (professional), Dale Olsen (blue-collar), Chris Tonks (white-collar)
> professional: Lee Faber (white-collar)

50. THE TRAVEL AGENTS

By clue 1, the New Yorker is not Kirk, Willy, or Toby; nor, by clue 2, is he Van or Hans; he is not Dino either (clue 5), so he is Yancy. Since Kirk visited him in March (clue 1), his 6-month

European tour must have begun in May, with Stockholm his first stop (clue 3), and run through October. By clue 1, Willy can have visited him only in November; the Parisian must have visited in December, Toby in April. Toby, then, is from Stockholm (clue 3), and Yancy visited him there in May. The Londoner is neither Kirk nor Willy (clue 1), Van nor Hans (clue 2); he is Dino. He did not visit Yancy in January (clue 1), so he visited in February after the Madrid friend in January. The Parisian is not Kirk or Willy (clue 1); and by clue 4, Van also cannot be the Parisian, who we know visited in December—the month after Willy—so Hans is the Parisian. Neither Van nor Willy is from Berlin (clue 4), so Kirk is. Willy is not from Madrid (clue 1), so Van is, and Willy is from Rome. By clue 5, then, Yancy visited London in July, and, by clue 6, Madrid in August—therefore Rome in June—and Berlin in October. By elimination, he must have spent September in Paris. In summary:

YANCY'S VISITORS	YANCY'S TOUR
January—Van from Madrid	May—Stockholm
February—Dino from London	June—Rome
March—Kirk from Berlin	July—London
April—Toby from Stockholm	August—Madrid
November—Willy from Rome	September—Paris
December—Hans from Paris	October—Berlin

51. WEDDING ANNIVERSARIES

The anniversary months include May but not August (clue 1); so, since they are five consecutive months, they are either January through May, February through June, or March through July. The five anniversary dates are as follows: Mrs. Williams is on the 10th or 20th, and Faith's is on the 30th (clue 2); Mrs. Dowling's is on the 7th or 21st (clue 6); Verity's is on the 16th or 25th (clue 7); the fifth, yet unnamed, woman's is on the 31st (clue 5). Two anniversaries are less than ten days apart, and neither is the one on the 31st (also clue 5); the second must be *before* the 10th of the month, and the only possible date of those listed is the 7th, so that is Mrs. Dowling's date. Even if Verity's date were the 25th of the shortest month, February, it would be at least 10 days to the 7th of the next month; so the only possible dates less than 10 days apart are Faith's on the 30th of one month and Mrs. Dowling's on the 7th of the following month. Hope, whose anniversary comes earliest in the year (clue 4), cannot be Mrs. Dowling; nor, since her date is before the 20th of the month (also clue 4), can she be the woman whose date is the 31st—so she can only be Mrs. Williams, and her date is the 10th. Prudence, whose anniversary is exactly 36 days after Mrs. Lawton's (clue 3), cannot be Mrs. Dowling, since the latter's date, the 7th, is directly after a month (Faith's) of at least 30 days, for a total of at least 37 days after the anniversary preceding Faith's. Thus, Prudence must be the one with the anniversary on the 31st and Mrs. Dowling, by elimination, is Constance. Mrs. Lawton cannot be Faith (the 30th and 31st can never be 36 days apart), so she must be Verity; the 16th of one month and the 31st of the next cannot be 36 days apart, so Verity Lawton's date is the 25th. Verity's anniversary, then, is on the 25th of one month, and Prudence's on the 31st of the following month. In order for them to be precisely 36 days apart, Verity's must be in a 30-day month (5 + 31 = 36). Since Prudence's anniversary is not in July (clue 3), the only possibility is that it is in May and Verity Lawton's in April. If Hope's anniversary, the earliest, is in January, then Faith's would be in February—impossible, since Faith's is on the 30th of the month. We have established by clue 5 that Faith's and Constance's anniversaries are in consecutive months, so those months can only be June and July. Thus, Hope's anniversary must be in March. Mrs. Swanson, who is not Faith (clue 8), is Prudence, and Mrs. Newman is Faith, In summary:

Hope Williams, March 10
Verity Lawton, April 25
Prudence Swanson, May 31
Faith Newman, June 30
Constance Dowling, July 7

52. THREE BY THREE

One family consists of Carol and her brothers, one of whom is a pilot (clue 4). A second family consists of Betty, her brother the copilot, and another sister (clue 5). Because five women's and four men's names are mentioned, the third family also consists of two women and one man. By clue 2, Helen must be one of the women in the third family, and her brother is a flight attendant—and since there is only one flight attendant in each family (clue 7), Ida's sister, who is also a flight attendant, can only be Betty. Ida is then a pilot (clue 5). Helen's sister, by elimination, is Ethel. By clue 3, Helen is a copilot. Carol and her brothers are then the Meltons (clue 6), and since none of them is a copilot, David must be Betty's and Ida's brother (again, clue 3). George is Carol's brother (clue 1). His brother is not also a pilot (clue 4), so by clue 8, Ethel, like her sister, is a copilot, and their last name is Felton. Frank's sister the pilot (clue 1) must be Carol, and Frank is a flight attendant (clue 7). By elimination, Betty, Ida, and David are the Peltons, and the third Felton triplet is Arthur. In summary:

> Feltons: flight attendant Arthur, copilot Ethel, copilot Helen
> Meltons: pilot Carol, flight attendant Frank, pilot George
> Peltons: flight attendant Betty, copilot David, pilot Ida

53. THE NEW APARTMENTS

Three men and three women are mentioned. No man's apartment is directly over another man's (clue 10), so the men aren't all on the same side of the building; therefore, neither are the women. Two women's apartments face the street (clue 6), so the other front apartment is a man's; again by clue 10, two men must occupy 1B and 3B in the back with a woman in 2B between them. Apartment 2A is also occupied by a woman (clue 4); that is, women share the second floor. Neil lives on the third floor, and one of the second-floor women is named Gorman (clue 5). That woman isn't Kay (clue 9), and Kay shares her floor, which isn't the third, with someone named Forney (clue 3); Kay's apartment can only be 1A, while Forney must be the man in 1B. The man in 3B is then Peter (clue 7), and Neil is in 3A; Forney, by elimination, is Mike. Gorman's apartment is then 2B (again, clue 5). Peter, in 3B, must be Dutton (clue 2). We now know the surnames of all those in the B line, so from clue 1, Lisa is in 2A, and Corwin is Kay in 1A. Gorman in 2B, by elimination, is Olivia. Since Lisa isn't Hill (clue 8), Neil is, and Lisa is Endicott. In summary:

> 1A, Kay Corwin
> 1B, Mike Forney
> 2A, Lisa Endicott
> 2B, Olivia Gorman
> 3A, Neil Hill
> 3B, Peter Dutton

54. THE TALENT SHOW

By clue 1, the ten children, in ascending order of age (and thus grade), are: (1) Randy's child; (2) Kathy Irons; (3) Steve and Monica's daughter, who has a sister; (4) and (5), the Jones boys; (6) a Gaines child; (7) Pam's daughter; (8) Sally, who has a sister; (9) Pam's other child, a boy; and (10) Ted's son. Reading through the introduction and clues, we find that there are five girls and five boys among the ten children. We know that the Jones children are both boys, and that Pam has both a son and a daughter. Nancy also has both a son and a daughter (clue 2). That accounts for four of the boys, so the fifth boy must have a sister, and the remaining family has two girls—so Steve and Monica's third-grader, who has a sister, and eighth-grader Sally, who also has a sister, must *be* sisters, as among the five families there is only one set of sisters. We know both the ninth- and tenth-graders are boys; thus, by clue 3, Sally's surname is Hughes, and the first-grader is Alice. By clue 5, then, Bob is in fifth grade, Jimmy is in sixth, and (since we know Kathy is in second) Chuck is in tenth. The fourth-grader is Bob Jones's brother, so John, who has a sister (clue 7), can only be Pam's son, and Bob's brother, by elimination, is Mike. Wayne's daughter, Cheryl (clue 6), must be John's sister. The younger Hughes girl, by elimination, is Cindy. Jimmy Gaines's sister can only be Randy's daughter, Alice, while Kathy Irons's brother can only be

Ted's son, Chuck. By elimination, Mr. Jones is Vic, and Cheryl and John are the Keyes children. Nancy has a son and a daughter but is not Mrs. Gaines (clue 2), so she is Mrs. Irons. Nor is Olive Mrs. Gaines (clue 4), so she is Mrs. Jones, and Mrs. Gaines is Linda. In summary:

Randy & Linda Gaines: Alice (1st) & Jimmy (6th)
Steve & Monica Hughes: Cindy (3rd) & Sally (8th)
Ted & Nancy Irons: Kathy (2nd) & Chuck (10th)
Vic & Olive Jones: Mike (4th) & Bob (5th)
Wayne & Pam Keyes: Cheryl (7th) & John (9th)

55. NEW CAREERS

Jody and Ms. Field, who both have young children, share an apartment on Oak Street (clue 1). From clue 4, Marge is married with grown children, has nursing training, and is not Ms. Holt or Ms. Smith. She cannot be Ms. Field on Oak (clue 1), the divorced woman on Tenth (clue 5), or Ms. King (clue 11); she must be Ms. Wilks. She doesn't live on Elm (clue 2), so she lives on Maple. By clue 8, then, she is studying to be a medical technician. Ruth, who does not live on Tenth or have young children (clue 7), must be the widow on Elm Street (clue 2). Jody (clue 1) cannot be either Ms. Field or the divorced woman on Tenth Street, so Claudia and Ginny must be, in some order. If Ginny is Ms. Field, Claudia must be Ms. King (clue 9), who works at a day-care center and lives on Tenth (clue 5). Since Claudia King could not have experience in nursing, nutrition (clue 11), typing (clue 9), or finances (clue 6), she must have experience in club work. However, this contradicts clue 10. So Claudia must be Ms. Field on Oak Street, and Ginny must work at the day-care center and live on Tenth. Since Ginny must be either Ms. Holt or Ms. Smith (clue 11), she cannot have typing experience (clue 9), nor can she have club experience (clue 10) or financial experience (clue 6). She must have nutritional training. Claudia Field does not have typing experience (clue 9) or club experience (clue 10), so she must have the financial experience and now work as a bank teller (clue 6). Since Ms. Holt and Ms. Smith do not have typing experience (clue 9), Ms. King must. Ms. King is divorced (clue 9), so she is not Ruth and must be Jody. By clue 3, Ruth must sell real estate and, by elimination, she must have club experience. She is not Ms. Smith (clue 10), so she is Ms. Holt, and Ginny is Ms. Smith. Jody is taking a paralegal course. In summary:

Claudia Field, Oak St.: family finances, bank teller
Ruth Holt, Elm St.: club work, real estate
Jody King, Oak St.: typing, paralegal course
Ginny Smith, Tenth St.: nutrition, day care
Marge Wilks, Maple St.: nursing, med. tech. course

56. TOPICS FOR DISCUSSION

From clues 1 and 4, current events are discussed on Monday, Wednesday, and Friday, and the boys like these days best; they dislike Tuesday, Wednesday, and Thursday. There are two girls, then, who like Tuesday and Thursday and dislike Monday and Friday. Local current events is Wednesday's topic (clue 6); national and foreign events are respectively on Monday and Friday (clue 4). "Morality in Everyday Life," the Fisher girl's favorite, is Thursday, and "Conservation" Tuesday (clue 2). Val likes Monday least and is a girl, and the Abbot boy likes Tuesday least (clue 7). The Abbot boy's favorite day can't be Monday or Friday (also clue 7), so it is Wednesday, while Val's is Tuesday. Val's most- and least-liked days are consecutive, so her last name is not Drew (clue 5); nor is it Parker (clue 2), so it is Nelson, and the Fisher girl dislikes Friday. From clue 7, the boy who dislikes Wednesday is the same one whose favorite is Friday, so the other boy likes Monday and dislikes Thursday; these two are, in one order or the other, Pat and the Drew boy (clue 5), and Pat's last name is Parker. If the Fisher girl were Lee, then, by clue 3, Chris would be the boy who dislikes Wednesday—and whose favorite day would immediately follow the Fisher girl's, contradicting clue 8. Lee is therefore the boy who dislikes Thursday and likes Monday—and must be the Drew boy—while the Abbot child is Chris. Pat Parker is then the boy who likes Friday and dislikes Wednesday. The Fisher girl, by elimination, is Fran. In summary:

Mon.: national current events; liked by boy Lee Drew, not by Val Nelson
Tues.: "Conservation"; liked by girl Val Nelson, not by Chris Abbot
Wed.: local current events; liked by boy Chris Abbot, not by Pat Parker
Thurs.: "Morality in Everyday Life"; liked by girl Fran Fisher, not by Lee Drew
Fri.: foreign current events; liked by boy Pat Parker, not by Fran Fisher

57.   THE TOP FIVE HITS

According to clue 4, "Age of Sagittarius" was not #1 either the first or second week, nor could it have been #1 the fourth or fifth week since it could not have been in second place in the fifth week (clue 5), so it was #1 the third week and #2 the first week. "Evening Has Shattered" was not #1 the first week (clue 3), so, by clue 1, it must have been #3 and "Beverly's Song" was #4; "Tiptoe Through the Violets" was not #1 (clue 5), so it was #5, and "Burning Chariots" was #1. "Evening Has Shattered" was not #1 the fourth week (clue 3) or fifth week (clue 6), so it must have been #1 the second week. By clue 5, "Age of Sagittarius" must have been either #4 or #5 the fifth week. Since "Burning Chariots" was one place higher than "Evening Has Shattered" that week (clue 6)—i.e., they were respectively either #3 or #4, or #4 and #5—the only possibility is that "Burning Chariots" was #3, "Evening Has Shattered" #4, and "Age of Sagittarius" was #5. "Age of Sagittarius" was then #4 the fourth week (again, clue 5), and, by elimination, #3 the second week. "Tiptoe Through the Violets," which we know was #5 the first week, must have then been #4 the second week (clue 5) and #3 the third week (clue 2). By elimination, #3 the fourth week was "Beverly's Song," and #4 the third week was "Burning Chariots." "Burning Chariots" must have been #5 the fourth week, and "Evening Has Shattered" was #2 (clue 6); "Tiptoe Through the Violets" was then #1 that week. By elimination, the fifth week, "Beverly's Song" was #1 and "Tiptoe Through the Violets" was #2; the second week, "Burning Chariots" was #2 and "Beverly's Song" #5; the third week, "Beverly's Song" was #2 and "Evening Has Shattered" #5. In summary:

	#1	#2	#3	#4	#5
Week 1:	"Burning Chariots"	"Age of Sagittarius"	"Evening Has Shattered"	"Beverly's Song"	"Tiptoe Through the Violets"
Week 2:	"Evening Has Shattered"	"Burning Chariots"	"Age of Sagittarius"	"Tiptoe Through the Violets"	"Beverly's Song"
Week 3:	"Age of Sagittarius"	"Beverly's Song"	"Tiptoe Through the Violets"	"Burning Chariots"	"Evening Has Shattered"
Week 4:	"Tiptoe Through the Violets"	"Evening Has Shattered"	"Beverly's Song"	"Age of Sagittarius"	"Burning Chariots"
Week 5:	"Beverly's Song"	"Tiptoe Through the Violets"	"Burning Chariots"	"Evening Has Shattered"	"Age of Sagittarius"

58.   DEAL OF THE CARDS

The four corner cards are the jack of hearts, the jack of clubs, the queen of diamonds, and the ace of clubs (clue 2). Card 1 is therefore either the jack of clubs or the ace of clubs (clue 6), and neither card 4 nor card 13, therefore, can be a club (clue 3). Cards 4 and 13 are then, in one order or the other, the queen of diamonds and the jack of hearts, and card 16 is either the ace of clubs or the jack of clubs. Card 4 cannot be the queen of diamonds (clue 7), so it is the jack of hearts, and card 13 is the queen of diamonds. Therefore card 16 cannot be the jack of clubs (clue 4), so it is the ace of clubs, and card 1 is the jack of clubs. Card 12 is not a diamond (clue 8), so it is a spade, and card 8 is a diamond (clue 3). By clue 4, cards 8 and 12 are, in one order or the other, a king and a queen; we have already placed the queen of diamonds, so card 8 is the king of diamonds, and card 12 is the queen of spades. By clue 3, card 5 must be a spade, and card 9 is therefore a heart. Since the second row has no aces in it (clue 5), by clue 4, card 5 is the king of spades and card 9 the ace of hearts. Card 2 is not a spade (clue 9), so, by clue 3, card 3 is a spade and card 2 a diamond, while card 14 is a spade and card 15 a heart. The aces of diamonds and spades are both on the periphery (clue 1), so the ace of diamonds can only be card 2; by clue 4, the ace of spades cannot be card 14 and is therefore card 3. We have placed the ace, king, and queen of spades, so card 14 is the jack of spades. We have placed the ace and jack of hearts (cards 9 and 4), and a third heart (card 15); by clue 3, the remaining heart can only be card 6. Cards 7 and 10 are then clubs, card 11 the remaining diamond, the jack. Card 7 is the queen of clubs,

161

card 10 the king (clue 10). By clue 4, card 6 is the queen of hearts and card 15 is the king. In summary:

1: jack of clubs	9: ace of hearts
2: ace of diamonds	10: king of clubs
3: ace of spades	11: jack of diamonds
4: jack of hearts	12: queen of spades
5: king of spades	13: queen of diamonds
6: queen of hearts	14: jack of spades
7: queen of clubs	15: king of hearts
8: king of diamonds	16: ace of clubs

59. UP AND DOWN THE TENNIS LADDER

By clue 7, the man on rung #1 didn't lose to the man on rung #4. By clue 6, #3 didn't lose to #6. So, by clue 3, #2 lost to #5. Thus, #1 played either #3 or #4 (by the challenge rules). From clue 8, #1 must have played #4, and by clue 7, #1 was the winner of the match. By elimination and the challenge rules, #3 played #6; by clue 6, #3 was the match winner. Of the two remaining matches, involving the players on rungs 7 through 10, at least one was between players next to each other on the ladder, since, by clue 5, Edwards lost to a challenger one rung below him. Either #8 played #9 and #7 played #10, *or* #7 played #8 and #9 played #10. If the former, then Edwards was #8 before his match and #9 after it. But, by clue 6, this is not a possibility. So the second possibility is the true case: #7 played #8 and #9 played #10. By clue 5, Edwards, although a loser, was still a rung above someone after his match. Thus Edwards was #7, and by clue 2, the challenger to whom he lost, who had been in the #8 position, was Dennis. Thus far, we know: #1 defeated #4; #5 defeated #2; #3 defeated #6; #8 (Dennis) defeated #7 (Edwards); and #9 played #10 (winner yet to be determined). Forrest was #9 after the weekend matches (clue 5). The Brown–Case match, which resulted in a move down the ladder by Brown (clue 9) can only be the one in which #5 challenged and defeated #2. Since #1 and #3 defeated their challengers, the third man who lost to a challenger, Grey (clue 4), must have been #9 and must have lost to Forrest, then in the #10 position. The two losing challengers, #4 and #6, were, in one order or the other, Adams (clue 1) and Kane (clue 10); since Brown moved from #2 to #5, Adams was, and remained, #4 (clue 9), while Kane was, and remained, #6. Harris was, and remained, #1 (clue 1). By elimination, the one who defeated Kane to retain his #3 position was James. In summary:

	BEFORE	AFTER
#1	Harris	Harris (defeated Adams)
#2	Brown	Case (defeated Brown)
#3	James	James (defeated Kane)
#4	Adams	Adams
#5	Case	Brown
#6	Kane	Kane
#7	Edwards	Dennis (defeated Edwards)
#8	Dennis	Edwards
#9	Grey	Forrest (defeated Grey)
#10	Forrest	Grey

60. FATHER'S DAY SHIRTS

Two of the children are Billy and the Larson boy, both of whom gave their fathers long-sleeved shirts (clue 2). Only two boys are mentioned, so the Larson boy must be Jim and, from clue 7, Billy's last name is Harris. A third child, a girl, gave her father a shirt with French cuffs (clue 1). A fourth child is the Malone girl, who also gave her father a long-sleeved shirt (clue 4). The fifth child is then the girl who gave her father a short-sleeved shirt. By clue 2, since only three sleeve lengths are represented, one of the two boys gave his father a shirt with 33″ sleeves (i.e., the two sleeve lengths were either 32″ and 33″ or 33″ and 34″). The shirt with French cuffs had the same length sleeves as one of the shirts given by the boys, and there were no other duplications in measurements (clue 1). Thus, Mr. Malone's sleeve length, which is not 32″ (clue 4), cannot be 33″

and must be 34″. By clue 2, then, Mr. Harris's sleeve length is 33″ and Mr. Larson's is 32″; the sleeve length of the French-cuffed shirt is one of these two. The shirt Billy Harris bought had a smaller collar than the one Jim Larson gave his father (clue 2); its collar was also smaller than that of the one Emily bought (clue 7), so it measured no more than 15½″. The shirt with the 16″ collar and 33″ sleeves (clue 8), and we know bought by a girl, can only be the one with French cuffs. All the collar measures were different. By clue 7, if Emily's gift had a 16½″ collar, Billy Harris's had a 15½″ collar Jim Larson's would then have a 16″ collar (clue 2), the same as the French-cuffed shirt—so that is impossible. Emily's gift did not have a 15½″ collar, since that shirt was given by a boy (clue 9). Therefore, the only possibility is that Emily's gift was the shirt with the 16″ collar—i.e., the one with French cuffs—and Mr. Harris's collar size is 15″. The boy who gave his father a shirt with a 15½″ collar is then Jim. From clue 3, Mr. Powell can be only the one who received the short-sleeved shirt, and his collar size must be 14½″, while Gil is Emily's father. By elimination, Mr. Malone's collar size is 16½″, and Gil's last name is Schick. Ted's son isn't Jim (clue 9) and must be Billy; Kevin, who also has a son (clue 10), must be Jim's father. Linda's father isn't Mr. Malone (clue 5), so her surname is Powell; her father isn't Nick (clue 6), so Nick is Mr. Malone. By elimination, Nick's daughter is Mary and Linda Powell's father is Colin. In summary:

Ted Harris from Billy, 15″/33″
Kevin Larson from Jim, 15½″/32″
Nick Malone from Mary, 16½″/34″
Colin Powell from Linda, 14½″/short sleeves
Gil Schick from Emily, 16″/33″ (Fr. cuffs)

61. BRISTOL HIGH REUNION

Since five occupations and five avocations are mentioned, each is shared by precisely two people, and no husband and wife shared either. All five women are mentioned in clue 1, and at least four attended Bristol High; the fifth woman is an attorney. Clue 4 tells us that she is Betsy, she did not attend Bristol High, and she does not live in Bristol. We know that the hosts, the Franks, live in Bristol, as do the Ians (clue 2) and the Johnsons (clue 6). By clue 2, two of the couples—who must be the Greens and the Holts—stayed with the Ians, and attorney Betsy must be Neil's wife. Neil must be a Bristol High alumnus (else he and Betsy would not be attending the reunion). Therefore, from clue 7, he and Betsy are the Greens and the teacher and her husband are the Holts. Also from clues 7 and 8, Mr. Holt must be an artist. Mr. Johnson, like Betsy Green, is an attorney (clue 4). We have accounted for both attorneys, and only one is a woman—so Neil, who married her, is a bridge player (clue 1). From clue 3, Ozzie and the physician's wife are the amateur chefs, both of whom live in Bristol; so Ozzie and the physician are, in one order or the other, Mr. Frank and Mr. Ian. Les is not Mr. Johnson but he is also a Bristol resident (clue 6), so he is a physician, as is attorney Johnson's wife. The man who became a teacher is not bridgeplayer Neil (clue 1), so he is Ozzie. One woman became an artist and is not Mrs. Frank (clue 1); she is Mrs. Ian. By elimination, the two dentists are Mrs. Frank and Neil Green. The three women Neil dated in high school are Eve, artist Ian, and the bridge player (clue 1), Dr. Johnson isn't the bridge player (clue 6; we know Neil is a bridge player), so she is Eve, and teacher Holt is the bridge player. Ann is neither Mrs. Holt nor Mrs. Ian (clue 7); she is Dr. Frank, the dentist. Since Mrs. Holt is a bridge player, Max, who married a jogger (clue 5) must be attorney Johnson—and since Dr. Johnson is a jogger, so is physician Les (clue 6). Artist Holt must be Ken. Ann Frank is a dentist and Ken Holt an artist, so what they have in common is a hobby (clue 7); Ann is therefore not Les's wife, who shares Ozzie's hobby, so her husband is Ozzie, while Les is the husband of artist Ian. Les's wife isn't Cheryl (clue 3); she is Donna, and Cheryl is Mrs. Holt. There is a male tennis player, and he is not Max (clue 5); he is Ken Holt, and Ann Frank is also a tennis player (clue 7). The two golfers, by elimination, are Betsy Green and Max Johnson. In summary:

Ann (dentist, tennis) and Ozzie (teacher, chef) Frank
Betsy (attorney, golf) and Neil (dentist, bridge) Green
Cheryl (teacher, bridge) and Ken (artist, tennis) Holt
Donna (artist, chef) and Les (physician, jogger) Ian
Eve (physician, jogger) and Max (attorney, golf) Johnson

62. THE JAYS

We know from what Gig Bigbucks told Patty in the last paragraph that one and only one statement about June's instrument was true. Three such statements were made: two of the Jays, Jimmy and June herself, said she plays piano (clues 5 and 9); a third, Jeffrey, said that he and June both play violin (clue 11). Since only one of those can be true, Jeffrey's statement was the only true one, and neither Jimmy nor June was telling the truth. Since Jeffrey plays violin, Johnny's statement (clue 14) was true, and Jane plays piano. By clue 2, then, Jane told the truth, so Jeremy also plays piano while Jack plays guitar. Since the truth-tellers tell the truth consistently, Jane's other statement is also true, and she is sixteen (clue 10). We know Jeffrey told the truth—so his earlier statement about his age (clue 3) is also true; Jack, who made a contradictory statement (clue 1), was then not telling the truth. Since Jane is sixteen, Joy didn't tell the truth (clue 8). We now know that four of the nine—Jimmy, June, Jack, and Joy—did not tell the truth; since the majority did, that means all the other five did, including Jeremy and Joanne. Joy is eleven (clue 4), and Joanne and Joy both play drums (clue 12). Joanne is thirteen (clue 6), Johnny is twelve and plays the ukulele, and Jimmy plays guitar (clue 13). By clue 3, since Jeffrey told the truth and Joanne is thirteen, Jeffrey and Jimmy are both ten. Johnny also told the truth, so June, like Johnny, is twelve (clue 7). We know that Jane is sixteen and the oldest—i.e., she is the only sixteen-year-old. Joanne, who told the truth, said that three of the others are older than thirteen years (clue 6), so the other two must be Jack and Jeremy. Since the latter told the truth, by clue 4, Jeremy must be fifteen and Jack fourteen. In summary:

> Jack, 14: guitar
> Jane, 16: piano
> Jeffrey, 10: violin
> Jeremy, 15: piano
> Jimmy, 10: guitar
> Joanne, 13: drums
> Johnny, 12: ukulele
> Joy, 11: drums
> June, 12: violin

63. ZODIAC PAIRS

Jack's sign is Taurus (clue 1). Only two men, David Yates and the Piscean, caught six fewer fish than another (clue 3), so Robert's sign is Pisces (clue 4). And Rebecca's is Aries (clue 1). Since Robert caught only four fish, Mr. Sanford is the husband of the Moon Child (clues 3, 4). Ken's and Mary's signs are either Virgo or Libra (clue 1); but the Libran is a woman (clue 4), so she is Mary, and Ken's sign is Virgo. The Moon Child, Mrs. Sanford, is not Rachel (clue 2), Joyce or Anna (clue 4), so she is Doris. Since hers is a summer sign, her husband's is an autumn sign; we know Mary is Libra, and the Scorpio is also female (clue 2), so Mr. Sanford is the Sagittarian. He is not Donald (clue 3), so he is Doris's fellow astrology buff, Ron. Turning to the sunbathers (clues 2, 5), Arian Rebecca must be Mrs. Fleming, Anna's sign Scorpio. The Capricorn, a woman, is not Rachel (clue 2), so she is Joyce—and the Aquarian, also a woman (clue 4), must be Rachel. Arian Rebecca Fleming must be married to Piscean Robert, the only male of the winter signs. Mr. Hudson's first name is not Donald or Ken (clue 3), so he is Taurean Jack. Capricorn Joyce is married to a man with a spring sign. Since Jack Hudson caught 12 fish and Doris Sanford's husband caught 10 (clue 3), Joyce is not Jack's wife (clue 4) so her husband's sign is Gemini; by the same two clues, since Rebecca's husband, Robert, caught 4 fish, Joyce's husband is not David Yates; he must be Donald (and by elimination, David Yates's sign is Leo). Joyce and Donald are not the Winstons (clue 5), so they are the Richardses, and Winston is Ken's last name. Since Donald Richards caught eight fish, Anna is married to David Yates (clues 3, 4). Libran Mary must then be married to the man of the remaining summer sign, Virgo—i.e., Ken Winston. And Rachel is Mrs. Jack Hudson. In summary:

> Rebecca (Aries) and Robert (Pisces) Fleming
> Jack (Taurus) and Rachel (Aquarius) Hudson
> Donald (Gemini) and Joyce (Capricorn) Richards
> Doris (Moon Child) and Ron (Sagittarius) Sanford
> David (Leo) and Anna (Scorpio) Yates
> Ken (Virgo) and Mary (Libra) Winston

64.   AT THE SUPERMARKET

Six types of goods are listed, and each woman bought five items. From clue 1, six of the women bought all but one of the six possible types. Since no two women had the same combination of purchases, (also clue 1) each of the six omitted a different type: one bought one of everything except tomatoes, another one of everything except peas, etc. Of these six women, then, five bought onions. The other three did not (clue 3). Francine bought only milk and/or bread (clue 2), so she must be one of the women mentioned in clue 3. Since none of the women has a last name beginning with F, she must be Ms. Davis. She bought two quarts of milk (clue 6), so she must have bought three loaves of bread. We know that all five of the women who bought onions bought five *different* items. Ms. Ingersoll, who bought two cans of peas (clue 6), is then not one of those five, so she is one of those mentioned in clue 3 and, since none of the women's first names begins with I, she must be Helen. The third woman who bought no onions is Ms. Collins (clue 5), and she must be the one who bought one of everything else listed; her first name, by clue 3, is Cheryl. The five remaining women each bought five different items. Ms. Bailey bought one of everything except bread, Beatrice one of everything except milk (clue 4). Dana bought one of everything except tomatoes, Gina one of everything except peas (clue 5). The eighth woman bought one of everything except lettuce. Helen Ingersoll must be the third woman who bought no tomatoes (clue 5). Since Francine Davis bought only two types of merchandise, Helen must be the one referred to in clue 1 who bought four types—so in addition to her two cans of peas, she must have bought a loaf of bread, one quart of milk, and one head of lettuce. Ms. Bailey is married (clue 4), so Arlene, who is single (clue 7), must be the eighth woman, the one who bought one of everything except lettuce; Ms. Bailey, by elimination, is Evelyn. Ms. Graham, who is single, is not Arlene (clue 7)—and since Cheryl's last name is Collins, Ms. Graham is not Gina (clue 3). Nor is she Beatrice, who is married (clue 8), so she is Dana. Ms. Arnold is married (clue 7), but is not Beatrice (clue 8), so she is Gina. Ms. Edwards is also married (clue 7), so she must be Beatrice, and Arlene, by elimination, is Ms. Lewis, In summary:

	tomatoes	peas	bread	milk	lettuce	onions
Gina Arnold	1	0	1	1	1	1
Evelyn Bailey	1	1	0	1	1	1
Cheryl Collins	1	1	1	1	1	0
Francine Davis	0	0	3	2	0	0
Beatrice Edwards	1	1	1	0	1	1
Dana Graham	0	1	1	1	1	1
Helen Ingersoll	0	2	1	1	1	0
Arlene Lewis	1	1	1	1	0	1

65.   THE COMPANY PICNIC

We are told everyone brought spouse, child(ren), or both to the picnic. Those with only children, and no spouse, present took part only in the peanut relay; everyone else competed in the sack race. Chris, who was in more than one contest (clue 2), must have entered the sack race and one other. Since Lee wasn't in any event with Chris (clue 3), Lee wasn't in the sack race; that is, Lee's spouse wasn't present, and the event Lee won was his or her only event, the peanut relay. Chris then, was not in that contest (again, clue 3) and must have entered the beer-drinking contest as well as the sack race—and must be a man who brought his wife, but no children, to the picnic. Pat had the same number of family members present as Chris (clue 4)—i.e., one. Since there was no duplication of family among winners (clue 5), Pat is a woman who brought her husband, but no children. (If Pat's one family member had been a child, she would have qualified only for the peanut relay, and we know Lee won that.) Women didn't participate in the beer-drinking contest, so Chris won that, and Pat won the sack race. Since the winners of the sack race and the peanut relay were of opposite sexes (clue 1), Lee is a man. In summary:

Chris brought wife only, won beer-drinking contest
Lee, a man, brought child(ren) only, won peanut relay
Pat brought husband only, won sack race

66. MISPLACED PLACE CARDS

We are told that Paula had intended to sit at the north end of the table with her husband at the south end, but they ended up just reversed; and that she had intended to alternate men and women, and that is how they ended up—i.e., there were two men and two women on each side of the table. Mr. Truman's first name is not Jim (clue 3), Ken (clue 4), Mark (clue 7), or Bob (clue 9); it is John. Clue 2 states that Mr. and Mrs. Miller, Brenda, and Mr. Brown ended up on the west side of the table (to John's right). Nora, who is not Mrs. Miller (clue 7), must have sat on the east side. Mr. and Mrs. Washburn ended up next to each other (clue 5), so they could only have sat on the east side of the table. By elimination, the other man on the east side was Mr. Rockford. We know that men and women sat in alternating seats, so Mrs. Miller had to end up either to John Truman's immediate right *or*—if she was in the other west-side seat occupied by a woman—between her husband and another guest. Therefore, Amy cannot be Mrs. Miller (clue 3). Amy must have been one of the two women on the east side of the table and, since we know the Washburns sat next to each other, Amy is not Mrs. Washburn; Nora is. And since Amy didn't sit at John Truman's immediate left, the people who ended up on the east side of the table were, in order from north to south, Nora Washburn, Mr. Washburn, Amy, and Mr. Rockford; Amy thus cannot be Mrs. Rockford, so she is Mrs. Brown. By elimination, Brenda's last name is Rockford and Mrs. Miller's first name is Joan. By clue 4, Ken must have ended up at Paula Truman's immediate left. By clue 6, Joan Miller ended up just across from Amy Brown, and by elimination, Brenda Rockford ended up just across from Nora Washburn. By clue 1, Paula had intended to seat husbands and wives on opposite sides of the table. Therefore, by clue 7, Mark is not Mr. Brown, Mr. Miller, or Nora Washburn's husband and can only be Mr. Rockford. Mr. Washburn, who sat to Amy's immediate right, is Jim (clue 3). By elimination, Bob ended up just across from Jim. Since, by clue 4, Paula had intended for Ken to be opposite Mark Rockford, Ken isn't Mr. Brown (clue 7); he is Mr. Miller, and Mr. Brown is Bob. We know all the names now, as well as the final seating arrangement. Paula's plans had called for her to sit at the north end of the table, John at the south end. She had not intended Joan Miller (clue 6), Brenda Rockford, or Nora Washburn (clue 8) to sit immediately to John's left, so the woman she intended for that position was Amy Brown. Nora and Joan were meant to be on the same side of the table (clue 7), so that was to John's right (on the east side of the table), so Brenda Rockford should have been the other woman on the west side (two places to Amy's left); by clue 6, Nora should have been at John's immediate right, with Joan opposite Brenda. Paula had not intended to sit next to Bob Brown (clue 9), so by clue 7, he should have been between Nora and Joan, with Mark Rockford at Paula's immediate left. Ken Miller, then, should have been at her immediate right (clue 4) and Jim Washburn, by elimination, between Brenda and Amy. In summary:

INTENDED SEATING		ACTUAL SEATING	
Paula Truman		John Truman	
Ken Miller	Mark Rockford	Brenda Rockford	Nora Washburn
Brenda Rockford	Joan Miller	Bob Brown	Jim Washburn
Jim Washburn	Bob Brown	Joan Miller	Amy Brown
Amy Brown	Nora Washburn	Ken Miller	Mark Rockford
John Truman		Paula Truman	

67. EXECUTIVE SUITE

From the introduction, the twelve individuals rank as follows: the chief executive officer, president, treasurer, the vice-presidents (of whom there must be three who rank equally), the chief executive officer's secretary, the president's secretary, the treasurer's secretary, and three equally ranked vice-presidents' secretaries. From clue 1, Grace and O'Reilly, who are of equal rank and also outrank at least five others, must be vice-presidents; Townsend, who outranks both, must be a higher executive. Also by clue 1, John, who outranks only three of the twelve, must be the treasurer's secretary, while Barry is secretary to one of the vice-presidents, and Iris is also a secretary. O'Reilly is a man, as is the other vice-president, and their secretaries are women (clue 5). Thus, Barry is Grace's secretary. Since Evelyn outranks someone and is not the chief executive officer's secretary (clue 11), she is either the president's secretary or one of the executives. By clue 7, Markham is a male secretary but not John, the treasurer's secretary; nor, since he outranks at least one other (also clue 7) can he be Barry, who outranks no one. He is not the chief executive officer's secretary (clue 4), so can only be the president's secretary, so Evelyn must be one of the executives. By clue 6, Shaeffer is either the president or the treasurer, Patterson is either the treasurer or a vice-president, and David, who is not a vice-president, is secretary to either the chief executive officer or the president. We now know that two of the vice-presidents' secretaries are women. John and Barry are also secretaries, as is David, whose last name then must be Markham. Quinn, the sixth secretary, is a woman (clue 12) but not Kathryn, so Kathryn is an executive. She is outranked by Larry, who is not the chief executive officer (clue 3), so, since the two vice-presidents whose first names we don't yet know are both men, Kathryn is the treasurer, and Larry, who outranks, her, must be the president. Ms. Quinn, the chief executive officer's secretary, is not Carol or Frances (clue 4), so she must be Iris, and Carol and Frances are secretaries to the male vice-presidents. We now have all six secretaries' first names at least: Iris Quinn, David Markham, John, Barry, Frances, and Carol. Thus, Alan and Harold, by elimination, are executives, along with Larry, Kathryn, Grace, and Evelyn. Larry outranks Harold, whose last name is not O'Reilly (clue 3), so Harold is the other vice-president, and Alan's surname must be O'Reilly. Evelyn, by elimination, is the chief executive officer. Since we know the surnames of the two secretaries who outrank John—Quinn and Markham— Whitman and Van Buren are both executives (clue 2). Townsend (clue 1), Shaeffer, and Patterson (clue 6) are also executives, as is O'Reilly. So the other surnames—Yarborough, Norton, Robinson, and Upton—must be secretaries. Yarborough is not Barry and ranks below Norton (clue 8); Yarborough, then, must be either Frances or Carol, and Norton's first name is John. Robinson, a woman, is not Frances (clue 9), so she is Carol. She is not secretary to Alan O'Reilly (clue 13), so she is secretary to Harold. By elimination, Frances's last name is Yarborough, and she is secretary to Alan O'Reilly. Barry's last name must be Upton. The three top executives' surnames are Townsend (clue 1), Shaeffer, and Patterson (clue 6); since Shaeffer is not the chief executive officer but outranks Patterson (also clue 6), Townsend must be chief executive officer Evelyn, and Shaeffer is Larry, the president. Whitman is a woman who ranks below Patterson (clue 10), so she is Grace, and Kathryn is Patterson. By elimination, Harold's surname is Van Buren. In summary; with the name of his or her secretary following each executive's:

> Chief Exec. Off. Evelyn Townsend, Iris Quinn
> Pres. Larry Shaeffer, David Markham
> Treas. Kathryn Patterson, John Norton
> V-P Alan O'Reilly, Frances Yarborough
> V-P Harold Van Buren, Carol Robinson
> V-P Grace Whitman, Barry Upton

68. CIRCUS SIDESHOWS

Kim's date wasn't Barry (clue 5), Eddie, Ralph, Tom (clue 6), or Frank (clue 8), so he was Dick. Sue dated neither Eddie, Ralph, Tom (clue 6), nor Barry (clue 1), so she dated Frank. Jenny's date was neither Barry nor Tom (clue 1), nor, since she didn't see Medusa's act (clue 4), did she date Eddie, who did (clue 2); she dated Ralph.

Sue and Frank did not see Medusa's 2:30 performance, since they saw Medusa at the same time Kim and Dick were watching Illustro (clues 3, 6). Nor did they see the 1:00 performance (clue 9). Eddie did not see Medusa's 1:00 performance either, since he saw Medusa at the same time Kim and Dick were watching Brobdingnag (clues 2, 7). Therefore, by clue 9, Eddie and his date saw Medusa's act at 1:30, Sue and Frank at 2:00. Clue 2 then describes the 1:30 shows, so it was then that Linda and her date saw Illustro, Ralph and Jenny saw Azbesto, and Kim and Dick saw Brobdingnag. The last tells us that Ralph and Jenny saw Brobdingnag at 1:00 (clue 7).

Since Sue and Frank saw Medusa's 2:00 show, all the performances in clue 6 took place at that time, and it was then that Ralph and Jenny saw Zoro, Tom and his date saw Hercule, Eddie and his date saw Azbesto, and Kim and Dick saw Illustro—and Barry and his date must have been at the 2:00 performance of the one remaining sideshow, Brobdingnag.

So far as Ralph and Jenny go, we have accounted for their whereabouts at the first three performance times. Clue 1, in which they are also mentioned, must then describe the 2:30 shows, so it was at 2:30 that Barry and his date saw Azbesto, Tom and his date saw Brobdingnag, Sue and Frank saw Zoro, and Jenny and Ralph saw Hercule. Alice then saw Azbesto at 2:00 (clue 10), so she must have been Eddie's date. Tom's date was not Carol (clue 4), so she was Linda, and Carol was with Barry. We now know who saw four of the six sideshows at 2:30. The remaining two, Medusa and Illustro, must have been seen by Dick and Kim and by Eddie and Alice, not necessarily in that order. Since we know Eddie saw Medusa at 1:30, at 2:30 he saw Illustro, and since Kim and Dick saw Medusa (clue 4), they must have done so at 2:30. Since Sue and Frank saw Zoro at 2:30, Kim and Dick must have seen that act at 1:00 (clue 8), the only other time still open on their sideshow schedule. Barry and Carol saw Medusa (clue 4), and since other couples were watching that act at the later times, they must have seen it at 1:00. Eddie and Alice saw Hercule (clue 5), so it must have been at 1:00, the only remaining time slot on their agenda. Frank and Sue saw Hercule, too (also clue 5), so that's where they were at 1:30. And since we have accounted for five couples at 1:30, Barry and Carol must have been watching Zoro's performance then.

Finally, since Tom and Linda saw Illustro at 1:30, the only show they could have been watching at 1:00 was Azbesto's, and it was Sue and Frank who saw Illustro's act then. In summary:

	1:00	1:30	2:00	2:30
Barry-Carol	Medusa	Zoro	Brobdingnag	Azbesto
Dick-Kim	Zoro	Brobdingnag	Illustro	Medusa
Eddie-Alice	Hercule	Medusa	Azbesto	Illustro
Frank-Sue	Illustro	Hercule	Medusa	Zoro
Ralph-Jenny	Brobdingnag	Azbesto	Zoro	Hercule
Tom-Linda	Azbesto	Illustro	Hercule	Brobdingnag

69. SCHEDULES FOR SUBSTITUTES

Harris is the substitute for the first-period classes (clue 1), Gerson for the senior period (clue 2), Smith for the sophomore classes (clue 4), Karp in the third period (clue 5), Jones in the fifth period (clue 6), and Brown for the freshman classes (clue 7). Since only one substitute is assigned in any period, these are six different periods. There is no assigned substitute in the seventh period (clue 8). Since Gerson and Karp could exchange their substitute assignments (clue 3), Gerson is free in the third period, Karp in the senior-class period; each then teaches regularly in all the other periods. Jones is free during the remedial-classes period (clue 9), which, since all periods have been mentioned either by number or activity, must be the first, third, or seventh; he therefore teaches in the freshman, sophomore, and senior periods. He also teaches in the first period, as does Smith (clue 1), and Brown and Harris both teach sophomore classes regularly (clue 4). At this point, we know the seven different periods, either by activity or by number—the 1st, 3rd, 5th, 7th, freshman, sophomore, and senior. Since Brown teaches the sophomores regularly and substitutes in freshman classes, the second period, when he is free (clue 7), must be the senior-class period; he then teaches regularly in all the other periods. Since Gerson substitutes, and Karp and Brown are free in the senior-class period, Harris and Smith teach regularly then (clue 2); they also teach regularly in the fifth period (clue 6) and in the freshman classes (clue 7). We know each of the six teachers regularly teaches five classes a day; i.e., there are a total of thirty regular classes. Thus far, we know there are five in the first period, three senior classes, five sophomore classes, five in the fifth period, and five freshman classes, totaling 23. Four classes meet in the special-interest period (clue 10), so the remaining period has three classes. The one period in which exactly four classes meet is the seventh period, with the other two teachers free (clue 8), so that is the period in which the special-interest classes meet. Since we know that Brown, Gerson, and Karp are teaching then, and Jones's free period is the one in which the remedial classes meet (clue 9), Jones teaches in the seventh period and the two who are free then are Harris and Smith. Jones's free period can only be the third, so that is when the remedial classes meet. The two remaining teachers in the third period, by elimination, are Harris and Smith. We know Harris and Smith are free in the seventh period, Harris substitutes in the first period, and Smith substitutes in the sophomore-class period. By clue 8, then, the first period must be eighth-grade math, and the sophomore classes meet in the fourth period. By elimination, the juniors meet in the fifth period and the freshmen in the sixth period. In summary:

Period	Class	Brown	Gerson	Harris	Jones	Karp	Smith
1	Eighth	T	T	Sub	T	T	T
2	Senior	Free	Sub	T	T	Free	T
3	Remedial	T	Free	T	Free	Sub	T
4	Sophomore	T	T	T	T	T	Sub
5	Junior	T	T	T	Sub	T	T
6	Freshman	Sub	T	T	T	T	T
7	Special Interest	T	T	Free	T	T	Free

168

70. GROCERY SHOPPING

We know that, since there were 48 items sold and each couple bought the same number, each couple bought four of the six items checked out; no two couples bought the same combination of items; and no couple bought two of any one item. The Nelsons were waited on ninth and bought cereal, bread, orange juice, and bacon (clue 17); Mrs. Nelson is Diane (clue 24). The last three couples waited on also did not buy milk (clue 20), so the first eight couples did. Therefore by clues 1 and 24, the Vandells, who bought bacon, were waited on tenth and the Clarks eleventh. The Smiths must have been waited on last (clue 15), and they bought bread, orange juice, bacon, and eggs (clue 6). Since the Nelsons, Vandells, and Smiths all bought bacon, Allen is Mr. Clark (clue 15) and the Clarks bought orange juice, bread, cereal, and eggs. Joe must be Mr. Smith, while Nola is Mrs. Clark (clue 24). The couples waited on first, second, and fourth did not buy eggs (clue 13), nor did the Nelsons, so all the others did. The Macks bought no bread or cereal (clue 8). The Thompsons bought milk, bread, bacon, and eggs (clue 2), and so were just behind the couple who bought milk, bread, orange juice, and bacon—i.e., bread but no cereal (clue 10). We know the Smiths bought no cereal, and that makes four—so all the others, including the Vandells, did buy cereal; the Vandells' other purchase was orange juice (clue 3). The Nelsons, Clarks, and Smiths all bought bread. The other five couples who bought bread were the first five (clue 11). The Thompsons and the couple just before them were then in that group, and by clue 10, the Thompsons were fourth or fifth. But since the Thompsons bought eggs, they were not fourth (clue 13), and must have been fifth, with the no cereal or eggs couple fourth. From clue 10, then, Janet and her husband were second, Jack and his wife third, and Jill and her husband sixth. Since the first five couples all bought bread, the sequence in clue 4 tells us that the Bakers were no earlier than fourth—and since the surnames of the last four couples are known, the Stevenses were no later than eighth and the Bakers no later than fifth. We know the Thompsons were fifth. Therefore, by clue 4, the Bakers were fourth, Gary is Mr. Thompson, the sixth couple bought orange juice and bacon in addition to their milk and eggs, the Stevenses were seventh and Bill and his wife were eighth. The sixth couple, Jill and her husband, are the Macks (clue 8). We now know that the couples waited on fourth, fifth, sixth, and twelfth did not buy cereal, so all the others did. Bill and his wife then bought milk, cereal, eggs, and one other item; that was orange juice (clue 3). As previously noted, the first two couples bought no eggs, so the Olsons, who bought both bread and eggs (clue 25), are Jack and his wife. We know the first two couples bought milk, bread, and cereal, but no eggs, so one bought orange juice as the fourth item and the other bacon, and the eighth package of bacon was bought by the Stevenses. The third through twelfth couples all bought bacon, eggs, or both, so by clue 5, Sue and her husband were first and their fourth item was orange juice, while Janet and her husband bought bacon. The seventh couple, the Stevenses, bought bacon, so by clue 18, Adam is Sue's husband and Janet is Mrs. Johnson. Bill and his wife bought eggs, so Adam and Sue must be the Ameses and Bill and his wife the Wickers (clue 21). The only possibilities fitting clue 19 are the Wickers, the Clarks, and the Vandells, so Steve is Mr. Vandell. Chuck is therefore Mr. Nelson (clue 12). Carol and Nikki can only be Mrs. Baker and Mrs. Thompson (clue 26). By clue 16, Sally is Mrs. Stevens and John is Mr. Mack; therefore, George must be Sally's husband (clue 23). Fern is Mrs. Wicker (clue 9), Mary is Mrs. Vandell (clue 14), and Judy is Mrs. Olson (clue 22); by elimination, Amy is Mrs. Smith. Tom must be Mr. Baker (clue 7) and Bob, by elimination, is Mr. Johnson. In summary, in the order waited on:

  1st Sue and Adam Ames—milk, orange juice, bread, cereal
  2nd Janet and Bob Johnson—milk, bread, cereal, bacon
  3rd Judy and Jack Olson—milk, bread, cereal, eggs
  4th Carol and Tom Baker—milk, orange juice, bread, bacon
  5th Nikki and Gary Thompson—milk, bread, eggs, bacon
  6th Jill and John Mack—milk, orange juice, eggs, bacon
  7th Sally and George Stevens—milk, cereal, eggs, bacon
  8th Fern and Bill Wicker—milk, orange juice, cereal, eggs
  9th Diane and Chuck Nelson—orange juice, bread, cereal, bacon
  10th Mary and Steve Vandell—orange juice, cereal, eggs, bacon
  11th Nola and Allen Clark—orange juice, bread, cereal, eggs
  12th Amy and Joe Smith—orange juice, bread, eggs, bacon

Clues 1, 2, and 3 group the pet owners by their pets' colorings: the four black pets are owned by Chita, Setter, Tom, and Wolf; the four white ones are owned by Bob, Cathy, Kitty, and Mr. Doggy; and the four spotted ones are owned by Felix, Kate, Rex, and Tab. We are missing only three first names in this list: Dane, Kathy, and Kit. Doggy, who is a man, can only be Dane. Kathy's surname isn't Setter (clue 5), so it is Felix, and Kit is Setter. Dane Doggy's pet is Empress (clue 4). By clue 9, Kate's, Kitty's, and Tab's last names are, in one order or another, Fox, Lynx, and Manx. Manx is a man (clue 10) and must be Tab. Kate's last name isn't Lynx (clue 5), so it's Fox, and Kitty is Lynx. Cathy owns a cat, Chita a dog (clue 12). Kathy Felix and Kate Fox both own cats (clue 5), so the other two owners of spotted pets, Rex and Tab, are both dog owners. Tab Manx's dog is male (clue 10), so Rex's is female. Kitty Lynx then also owns a female dog (clue 8); since we know Dane Doggy's pet is female, Empress is a cat, and the other two owners of white pets, Bob and Cathy, own males—and since we know Cathy has a cat, Bob owns a dog. We know Kitty's dog is female; by clue 6, King can only belong to Kathy Felix, so Kate Fox's cat is a female. From clue 13, Duke is a spotted dog and Duchess a spotted cat, so they are owned, respectively, by Tab Manx and Kate Fox. Tom then owns a cat (clue 14). We know the white female cat is Empress; the other white animals are Baron, Baroness, and Prince (clue 15), so Baroness is Kitty Lynx's female dog. Princess and Queen are both black (clue 16); the only female name left for Rex's spotted dog is Countess, and the remaining pet names—Count and Emperor—must belong to black animals. There is no surname ending with ''C,'' so by clue 11, Rex's last name ends with S and must be Mews. We know Count is black, and he is a cat (clue 12), so—since we know Chita owns a dog—by clue 17, he belongs to either Tom or Wolf, whose surname must be Chow; that person is not Tom (clue 7), so Count's owner is Wolf Chow. Tom's cat is then female, and Kit Setter, by elimination, owns a dog. We know Baron is a white animal, so he belongs to either Bob or Cathy. But his owner's surname is Barker (clue 17), who cannot be Bob (clue 4), so Baron's owner is Cathy Barker. Bob's dog, by elimination, is the remaining white animal, Prince. Chita is the only woman whose last name we haven't established; by clue 11, she is Ms. Wolfe and her pet's name either begins or ends with the letter E. That can only be Emperor, so Kit Setter's dog is female. Bob's last name isn't Lyon (clue 7); that must be Tom's surname, and Bob's is Katz. Tom Lyon's cat isn't Queen (clue 11); she is Princess, and Queen is Kit's dog. In summary:

Cathy Barker: white cat, Baron
Wolf Chow: black cat, Count
Dane Doggy: white cat, Empress
Kathy Felix: spotted cat, King
Kate Fox: spotted cat, Duchess
Bob Katz: white dog, Prince
Kitty Lynx: white dog, Baroness
Tom Lyon: black cat, Princess
Tab Manx: spotted dog, Duke
Rex Mews: spotted dog, Countess
Kit Setter: black dog, Queen
Chita Wolfe: black dog, Emperor

72. THE NINE MUSES

From the introduction, dancers 1, 2, and 3 stood at the left, dancers, 4, 5, and 6 downstage center, and dancers 7, 8 and 9 at the right. Dancer 5 was Terpsichore; as principals, she, dancer 2, and dancer 8 each stood between two attendants. Clue 1 describes all three groups. In one, Kathy was the principal between whoever played Thalia (comedy) and Ms. Rush as Melpomene (tragedy). In another, principal Bonnie was between June as Calliope (epic poetry) and Ms. Stone as Erato (lyric poetry). In the third, principal Ms. Lyman was between whoever played Polyhymnia (religious music) and Gwen. Of these nine dancers, the dancer whose full name is Fran White (clue 2), can only be Thalia or Polyhymnia, both attendants. The introduction tells us pairs of dancers exited in this order: attendants 1 and 9, principals 2 and 8, attendants 3 and 7. Attendants 4 and 6 would have exited together for a third curtain call, but the need did not arise (clue 4), so dancers 3 and 7 were the last to exit. By clue 2, Euterpe exited with Fran White, but not last; since Fran was an attendant, Euterpe must have been also, and they must be dancers 1 and 9. From the list in clue 1, Euterpe (secular music) can only be attendant Gwen, so she and Polyhymnia attended Ms. Lyman at one side of the stage, while Fran White as Thalia and Ms. Rush as Melpomene attended Kathy on the other side. We now know which six muses were attendants, so the two (in addition to Terpsichore), played by principal dancers were Clio (history) and Urania (astronomy). If Fran were dancer 1, Kathy would be 2 and Melpomene 3, contradicting clue 3; so Fran was 9, Kathy 8, and Ms. Rush 7. Gwen as Euterpe, Ms. Lyman, and Polyhymnia were respectively 1, 2, and 3. By clue 4, Holly and Ms. Vass were 4 and 6, in some order, so the downstage group was Bonnie as Terpsichore, June Vass as Calliope, and Holly Stone as Erato. We know that principals Ms. Lyman (dancer 2) and Kathy (dancer 8), who exited together, performed Clio and Urania, in some order. By clue 6, Ms. Young and Alice exited together, but neither played Urania, so they must be dancers 3 and 7; Alice is Ms. Rush (dancer 7), and Ms. Young portrayed Polyhymnia (dancer 3). We know the last of the three pairs to exit were Ms. Rush and Ms. Young. Fran White (dancer 9) and Gwen (dancer 1) were first, Kathy (dancer 8) and Ms. Lyman (dancer 2) second. By clue 5, then, Ms. O'Hara must be Gwen, and Kathy is Ms. Norton. Bonnie's surname, by elimination, is Quinn. Ms. Lyman, who exited with Kathy Norton, isn't Dana (also clue 5), so she is Ingrid, and Ms. Young is Dana. Ingrid Lyman played Clio and Kathy Norton, Urania (again, clue 5). Ingrid Lyman as Clio was dancer 2 in the group at the left; by clue 7, June Vass as Calliope was dancer 6 at right of center, and Holly Stone as Erato was dancer 4. In summary:

Calliope: June Vass, 6
Clio: Ingrid Lyman, 2
Erato: Holly Stone, 4
Euterpe: Gwen O'Hara, 1
Melpomene: Alice Rush, 7
Polyhymnia: Dana Young, 3
Terpsichore: Bonnie Quinn, 5
Thalia: Fran White, 9
Urania: Kathy Norton, 8

73. JOB INTERVIEWS

Faith's interview with Dr. Adams was at 2:00 (clue 9). Gloria's 1:00 appointment was with Dr. Davis (clue 13), so she saw Dr. Adams at either 10:00 or 11:00 (clue 10). If Gloria saw Dr. Adams at 10:00, she must have seen Dr. Cramer at 9:00, 11:00 or 2:00. By clue 4, she did not meet with him at 2:00; nor, also by clue 4, could she have met with him at 11:00, since there is no appointment set one hour later. Therefore, she would have to meet with Dr. Cramer at 9:00. However, then Dr. Adams would have to be the Fallriver superintendent (also clue 4), which contradicts clue 16. Thus Gloria must have met with Dr. Adams at 11:00. Gloria is not the biology major (clue 15), so by clue 1, the biology major must have met with Dr. Adams at 9:00 while Gloria is Ms. Owens. Again by clues 4 and 16, Gloria did not see Dr. Cramer at 10:00, so she saw him at 9:00. Helen isn't Ms. Mason (clue 6), so Faith is. By clue 6, since we know Faith saw Dr. Adams at 2:00, Helen and Faith saw Dr. Barnes at either 9:00 and 10:00 or 10:00 and 11:00, respectively. Since Dr. Barnes saw either Faith or Helen at 10:00, Gloria could not have seen him then; therefore he cannot be from Fallriver (clue 4). Dr. Evans, by elimination, must be, and Gloria saw him at 10:00. Her last appointment must have been with Dr. Barnes at 2:00. Dr. Barnes's 1:00 appointment was not with Ian (clue 2), so it was with chemistry major John (clue 5). Nor did he meet with Ian at 9:00 (again, clue 2)—so, by clue 6, he saw Helen at 9:00, Faith Mason at 10:00, and Ian at 11:00. From Dr. Adams's schedule thus far, we know the biology major isn't Gloria or Faith and was with Dr. Adams when Helen was with Dr. Barnes—and so must be Ian. By clue 12, Faith's 1:00 appointment wasn't with Dr. Cramer, so it was with Dr. Evans. At 1:00, when John was with Dr. Barnes, Dr. Adams must have met with Helen; he then saw John at 10:00. By elimination, in the 1:00 time slot, that is when Ian met with Dr. Cramer. Since Gloria was with Dr. Evans at 10:00, Ian was with Dr. Davis; Ian was with Dr. Barnes at 11:00, so by clue 2, Dr. Davis is from Autumnton. By elimination, Helen met with Dr. Cramer at 10:00. Faith was with Dr. Adams at 2:00, so Dr. Cramer saw her at 11:00 and John at 2:00. Faith's 9:00 appointment, the one remaining in her schedule, was thus with Dr. Davis, and John's 9:00 appointment was with Dr. Evans. Ian's first four appointments have been accounted for, so he is the one who saw Dr. Evans at 2:00. By elimination, Dr. Evans saw Helen at 11:00, while Dr. Davis saw John at 11:00 and Helen at 2:00. John, who was with Dr. Davis of Autumnton at

171

11:00, isn't Keller (clue 8); nor is Helen (clue 3), so Ian is. By clue 14, the Springdale superintendent met with the English major one hour before interviewing Long, who is either Helen or John. Dr. Adams saw John at 10:00, an hour after biology major Ian, and Helen at 1:00; Dr. Barnes saw Helen at 9:00 and John at 1:00. So Dr. Cramer is the one from Springdale and, since he saw John just after biology major Ian, Long is Helen and the English major is Gloria Owens. John's last name, by elimination, is Newman. Dr. Adams, whose three morning appointments were with the biology, chemistry, and English majors, is not from Summerset (clue 7); he is from Winterhaven, and the Summerset superintendent is Dr. Barnes. Dr. Adams's 2:00 appointment was with Faith Mason, so she isn't the math major (clue 11); her major is French, and Helen's is math. In summary:

	Dr. Adams Winterhaven	Dr. Barnes Summerset	Dr. Cramer Springdale	Dr. Davis Autumnton	Dr. Evans Fallriver
9:00	Ian Keller biology	Helen	Gloria	Faith	John
10:00	John Newman chemistry	Faith	Helen	Ian	Gloria
11:00	Gloria Owens English	Ian	Faith	John	Helen
1:00	Helen Long math	John	Ian	Gloria	Faith
2:00	Faith Mason French	Gloria	John	Helen	Ian

74. AT THE FOOTBALL GAME

By clue 2, Pamela and the Queen girl were at diagonally opposite corners of the group of seats, as were the Connors boy and Ann; i.e., together these four occupied seats 101, 105, 401, and 405. Ann's last name is Fowler, and she and Pamela were at the two ends of the same row (clue 6), so the Connors boy and the Queen girl were at the two ends of the other row. By clue 10, then, one front-to-back group of four students—either seats 101 through 401, or 105 through 405—consisted of the Connors boy, an unknown student, the Holland boy, and Pamela; another group, also 101 through 401 or 105 through 405, had the Queen girl in the front row and Ann Fowler in the back row, with two other (as yet unknown) students directly between them. By clue 7, a third front-to-back group consisted respectively of Will, the Egan girl, the Owens boy, and George; since Roger was in seat 103 (clue 16), this group represented either seats 102 through 402 or seats 104 through 404. The Potter boy sat immediately behind Ted (clue 18)—so from clue 3, a fourth front-to-back group (again, either 102 through 402 or 104 through 404) consisted of the Long girl, Ted, the Potter boy, and the Davis girl. A boy was in seat 403 (clue 8). By clue 14, Louise Landry sat directly behind Mary, and there was one row between them; the only possibility is that Louise sat immediately in front of Ann Fowler, and Mary is the Queen girl. Ned, who sat at the other end of Louise's row, is the Holland boy (clue 6). The only other girl in Mary Queen's row is the Long girl, so the latter's first name is Sandra (clue 11). One student who sat in the first row has identical first and last initials (clue 1). That cannot be the Connors boy, since the only boy whose first name begins with C, Carl, wasn't in the first row (clue 5). Nor can it be Will, since the only surname beginning with W is a girl's (also clue 5). It must be Roger, whose last name is then Rider. By clue 11, therefore, the Connors boy is Larry, and Will's last name is Morris. The only two girls in the first row were Mary Queen and Sandra Long, so by clue 15, the Thompson girl was in the fourth row. Since we know the Davis girl is not in an end seat, the Thompson girl must be Pamela. There are ten boys and ten girls in all, and we have specifically placed nine boys; the tenth, the Boyd boy, was somewhere in the second row along with Ted (clue 4), so the student in seat 303 was a girl—and by clue 5, the only possibility is that she was the Wilson girl and that the boy in seat 403 was Carl. The latter's last name isn't Allen (clue 19), so, by clue 20, the Allen boy, who must be in the fourth row, is George, while Karen is the Egan girl. The Smith boy, who must have sat in the fourth row, as did Pamela Thompson (clue 15), is then Carl. The three boys in the first row were Larry, Will, and Roger, so by clue 12, Diane is the Davis girl and David, who was somewhere in the second row, must be the Boyd boy. We know that three of those in the second row were Ted, Karen Egan, and David Boyd; a fourth student in that row was the Iverson girl (clue 15). By clue 4, the fifth in that row was the Andrews girl, and the Iverson girl's first name is Jane; Ted's surname, by elimination, is Jackson. Since Jane Iverson sat immediately in front of a boy (clue 17), that boy can only be Ned Holland. Larry Connors's front-to-back group was not in seats 105 through 405 (clue 13), so Larry was in seat 101, Jane in 201, Ned in 301,

172

and Pamela in 401; Mary, Louise, and Ann were then, respectively, in seats 105, 305, and 405. The Owens boy isn't Frank (clue 19), so he is Bill, and Frank is the Potter boy. Bill wasn't in seat 302 next to Ned (clue 9), so he was in seat 304—and Will was thus in seat 104, Karen in 204, and George in 404. Sandra, Ted, Frank, and Diane were then, respectively, in seats 102, 202, 302, and 402. By clue 9, Beth can only be the Wilson girl in seat 303. The Andrews girl, by elimination, is Vicky. Vicky Andrews was in seat 203, David Boyd in seat 205 (clue 17). In summary:

101, Larry Connors	301, Ned Holland
102, Sandra Long	302, Frank Potter
103, Roger Rider	303, Beth Wilson
104, Will Morris	304, Bill Owens
105, Mary Queen	305, Louise Landry
201, Jane Iverson	401, Pamela Thompson
202, Ted Jackson	402, Diane Davis
203, Vicky Andrews	403, Carl Smith
204, Karen Egan	404, George Allen
205, David Boyd	405, Ann Fowler

75. HOUSEHOLD ORGANIZATION

By clue 1, each day of the week, one woman does cleaning and another does laundry, i.e., no two women clean, or do laundry, on the same day. On Fridays, the three women who are not doing cleaning or laundry do miscellaneous chores (clue 6), so all cooking and shopping are scheduled no later in the week than Thursday. Betty cooks on Mondays, Ellie on Tuesdays (clue 7). Betty cleans, Fanny does laundry, and Mrs. Pligh shops, in that order, on different days (clue 2), so Betty cleans on Tuesdays, Fanny does laundry on Wednesdays, and Mrs. Pligh shops on Thursdays. Connie and Mrs. Rintz clean on Mondays and Tuesdays (clue 5), so Connie is the one who cleans on Mondays, and Mrs. Rintz is Betty. We know none of the women does her cooking later in the week than Thursday. Mrs. Sayles does her laundry, miscellaneous chores, and cooking in that order, but *not* on three consecutive days (clue 3); she must do laundry on Mondays, cooking on Thursdays, and miscellaneous chores on either Tuesdays or Wednesdays. We know none of the women does shopping on Fridays. Since none does shopping on Tuesdays, either (clue 6), Mrs. Sayles must do her shopping on Wednesdays; she then does her miscellaneous chores on Tuesdays and her cleaning, by elimination, on Fridays. Mrs. Sayles's schedule matches neither Connie's, Ellie's, nor Fanny's, so she is the fifth woman, Debbie. We now know Betty's, Ellie's, and Debbie's Tuesday tasks. Since Fanny does laundry on Wednesdays, the one who does laundry on Tuesdays must be Connie, who then does miscellaneous chores on Fridays. We know the one who cleans on Fridays is Debbie, so Fanny also does miscellaneous chores on Fridays; and since Connie cleans on Mondays and Betty on Tuesdays (remember that only one woman does that chore each day), Fanny must do her cleaning on Thursdays. She doesn't shop on Tuesdays (again, clue 6), so she does that on Mondays and cooks on Tuesdays. Wednesday is the only day left for Ellie to do her cleaning. Debbie Sayles shops on Wednesdays; Mrs. Schein, who also shops on Wednesdays (clue 4), must be Connie—and her Thursday chore, by elimination, is cooking. Since Fanny cleans on Thursdays, the Mrs. Pligh who shops on Thursdays can only be Ellie. Fanny, by elimination, is Mrs. Mintz. Ellie, who cannot do laundry on Mondays—Debbie's laundry day—does laundry on Fridays; she then does her miscellaneous chores on Mondays. Betty is then the third woman who does miscellaneous chores on Fridays. We know everyone's Thursday chores but Betty's, so she can only be the one who does laundry that day and, by elimination, she shops on Wednesdays. In summary, with the chores for each woman given in order, from Monday through Friday:

Fanny Mintz: shopping, cooking, laundry, cleaning, miscellaneous
Ellie Pligh: miscellaneous, cooking, cleaning, shopping, laundry
Betty Rintz: cooking, cleaning, shopping, laundry, miscellaneous
Debbie Sayles: laundry, miscellaneous, shopping, cooking, cleaning
Connie Schein: cleaning, laundry, shopping, cooking, miscellaneous